MW01047315

FROM CHAINS TO CHANGE

A RENEWED CONSCIOUSNESS

CRYSTAL GITTENS-CABIE

From Chains to Change
A Renewed Consciousness

Copyright © 2018 by Crystal Gittens-Cabie

ISBN: 978-1674042602
Second Edition 2 3 4 5 6 7 8 9 10

DEDICATION

This book is dedicated to my patient, loving husband Anthony Cabie and my two amazing sons Nahshon and Azariah Cabie. Thank you for your love, support and patience. I love you and I like you, now and forever.

ACKNOWLEDGEMENTS

Thanks are in order for the following people who assisted in the developmental process throughout this book. My friend RB, a great person who motivated me to continue writing and enthusiastically polished my efforts. My good friend Dawud and my sister Rhonda, for their constant feedback and support. Mr. Michael Griffith for his knowledge, expertise and unwavering support in helping me to expand my research list in the book. My children, for their hours of patiently listening to the contents of the book and inquisitively bombarding me with questions regarding the information received, as those questions helped me to ensure I had all the areas covered. My mother, for teaching me that there is no dream out of reach. And finally, to all the people who will read this book and utilise its suggestions and teachings as a beacon to guide a way forward to a new level of consciousness, I acknowledge you all.

CONTENTS

If one is free at heart, no man-made chains can bind one to servitude, but if one's mind is so manipulated and controlled by the oppressor, then there will be nothing the oppressed can do to scare his powerful masters. —Steven Biko

PREFACE

I remember it as though it was yesterday. I woke up around 3 am with a Ferris wheel of words whirling around in my head, urging me to arise and put pen to paper. Not wanting to lose precious, much-needed rest, I pushed the words aside and without opening my eyes, once again surrendered to sleep.

About an hour later, I experienced the same haunting of the words in my head and felt that failure to commit them to paper would result in me forgetting them completely. I awoke, crawled out of my nice, warm bed, took up my trusty pen valued at $1.50 along with my notebook and proceeded to the living room where I wrote for about three hours.

During this time of writing, the flurry of words in my head acted like a herd of captured stallions that, at that moment, had found a way of escape. The words just bolted from my head onto the pages of the book, and I had no idea what I had written until I was completely finished.

Feelings of fear enveloped me, as I didn't really understand what happened, and I feared that I had gone insane and was probably ranting on paper like one would see a crazy person doing on the streets. However, I read what I had written and those were the words that resulted in me creating this book. The realisation that this book was a way of life for me long before it was captured in ink didn't dawn on me until a friend brought it to my attention and that revelation had me determined to witness its completion.

Prior to its creation, I was on a self-realisation excursion and the more I searched, the more knowledge I gathered and the more questions I had.

As I became more aware and informed, I made an unexpected yet extraordinary observation. I realised that I was not the only person who had these questions and concerns and was searching for answers as I had initially thought. I, however, now had some of the answers through my research and for those who didn't, I could share my knowledge with them and give those who didn't even know where to begin searching, some guidance. This was my motivation to continue writing. It was the prelude to me helping others find some direction, and it was my way of giving hope to the hopeless and a solution to the problems instead of an excuse.

Writing this book was an interesting peregrination all on its own. It took me to new places both literally and figuratively; it helped me overcome some fears as I realised that fear kept me in an incapacitated state for the most part. It challenged me to see things from a different perspective, which evoked a more positive attitude within me.

The whirlwind of emotions that coursed through me was at times unnerving to say the least. I experienced passion, as I would find myself writing for hours, neglecting people and food in an attempt to make recordings of the thoughts in my head. I experienced anger as I watched what seemed like history repeating itself and felt as though I was the only one who took notice of it. I experienced happiness at the erudition received and the positive impact that was made in the lives of people I met. As I shared this renewed way of thinking, people saw a different side of not only me, but also themselves. There were weeks that went by without me writing even a single letter.

There were times when I was too exhausted to think of another chapter or when I became overwhelmed and frustrated with the amount of research and simply stopped writing. Nevertheless, I never stopped researching, listening or walking around with my pen and notepad. I would sit for hours watching documentaries pertaining to my topics or listen to people talking as I rode buses or taxis. I would visit the homes of the elderly in my community and bombard them with questions and eventually someone would say something that triggered a switch in my head and I would continue writing.

The book was designed to engage the reader and propel them from a point of limited knowledge of self to a more comprehensive, elevated state of consciousness. The beauty about adapting to these teachings or following the suggestions is that it will not result in people being viewed as crazed fanatics with extreme opinions or behavioural patterns. The book is meant as a manifest of the way we should regard others and ourselves and achieve goals without making excuses for failure.

CHAPTER ONE

THE CHAINS

WHO ARE YOU?

As a dark-skinned person, have you ever wondered about your nationality as it was before the slave trade? What was the belief system that your forefathers subscribed to? What language did your ancestors speak and what language you would have been speaking had it has not been for the slave trade that came about and viciously ripped their identity from them?

I don't believe that the biggest mystery on earth is whether there are other life forms in the universe. And I know I am not alone when I say I believe the biggest mystery is the true identity of dark-skinned (black) people.

This then leads to the important question: "Who are we really?" Are we Egyptian, Ethiopian, Libyan, Canaanite or Israelite? In addition, we need to ascertain why it is that "black" people, over the years have been persecuted, enslaved and have had things so hard?

Also, we need to determine, as it is my opinion, why there is no togetherness, harmony or love among this race of people?

When we reminisce on our history, we recognise that "blacks" have dealt with slavery since the days of Ancient Egypt to this present day, a fact that has been proven both archaeologically and biblically.

Archaeological finds presented by Dr John H. Taylor, the curator of the Egypt Department of the British Museum in London reveals items that are carbon dated to show the Israelites' period of slavery in Egypt along with proof that the Israelites built cities.

The "Blacks" were the very same ones known as Israelites who were enslaved in Egypt by Pharaoh. Moses redeemed these Israelites from Pharaoh, and they returned to Israel.

After returning to Israel, they were then enslaved by the Syrians, taken to Assyria and were eventually freed. We refer to *II Kings 17: Verse 5: Then the king of Assyria came up throughout all the land, and went up to Samaria, and besieged it three years.*

Verse 6: In the ninth year of Hoshea the king of Assyria took Samaria, and carried Israel away into Assyria, and placed them in Halah and in Habor by the river of Gozan, and in the cities of the Medes.

After returning to Israel, the Babylonians, who were also known as the Ethiopians or the Cushites, again enslaved them and then eventually they were liberated. In *I Chronicles 9:1* we read: *So, all Israel was reckoned by genealogies; and, behold, they were written in the book of the kings of Israel and Judah, who were carried away to Babylon for their transgression.*

They returned to Israel and then the Persians enslaved them. They were eventually freed and returned to Israel. **Ezra 9:9:** *For we were bondmen; yet our God hath not forsaken us in our bondage, but hath extended mercy unto us in the sight of the kings of Persia, to give us a reviving, to set up the house of our God, and to repair the desolations thereof, and to give us a wall in Judah and in Jerusalem.*

The Greeks enslaved them on their return trip from Persia, and they were again liberated where they returned to Israel.

Then the Romans had their chance to enslave them. Now that's a lot of biblical slavery. Even Jeremiah had to ask in **Jeremiah 2:14:** *Is Israel a servant? Is he a home born slave? Why is he spoiled?*

Those who did not abscond were captured, enslaved again and were taken to be used as gladiators. This was referred to as being placed in the lion's den in the Bible.

Some Israelites escaped to places like Algeria, Morocco and Tunisia before General Pompey captured Jerusalem. Others fled to the south of Africa, where the Sahara Desert is located. The Romans had no jurisdiction in the southern parts of Africa and with the knowledge that they, the Israelites, could not be recaptured, they had a sense of security.

These Israelites were skilful people as they gleaned knowledge from each of their captors over the years and passed it on from generation to generation.

When they fled to the various parts of Africa where they could not be reached by the long arms of the Romans, they effectively built and managed well-maintained successful societies. These societies were made up of carpenters, doctors, generals, judges, jewellers, agriculturists, historians, etc. and the variety of skills among the people gave them the ability to create a very capable and efficient society.

Even though some may have chosen to live a simple lifestyle in separate communities, "black" people were not swinging on vines, discovered (as they were not lost) and as primitive as our school history books try to have us believe. Even before the 1400s, slavery was recorded in what was known as the Classical times and prevailed despite the fall of the Roman Empire.

A more classical style of slavery existed in the southern and eastern parts of Europe with it aiding the economy as trading across the Mediterranean and the Atlantic seas allowed slaves to appear in places like Italy, Southern France, Portugal and Spain before the discovery of the "New World" in 1492 by Christopher Columbus.

COLUMBUS AND THE NEW WORLD

Christopher Columbus, born in 1451, was an Italian explorer who claimed to have discovered the "New World" of the Americas and has been credited for establishing same for European colonisation.

Columbus visited Africa on many voyages and gained knowledge of the Atlantic currents. After being rejected by Portugal, Genoa and Venice for a three-ship voyage of discovery, Columbus took his request to the Spanish Monarchy in 1487.

King Ferdinand of Aragon and Isabelle of Castille finally granted his request in the year 1492 Columbus left Spain in his ships Nina, Pinta and Santa Maria to embark on his voyage.

After 36 days of sailing, he and his crew claimed the Bahamas for Spain, trading glass beads, cotton balls, glass and spears with the inhabitants of the island, all the while paying attention to the gold the friendly natives used to adorn themselves with.

Columbus and his sailors also visited other islands, which we know today as Cuba, Trinidad and Tobago and Haiti. In 1493, after returning to the Navidad Settlement in Hispaniola to find the sailors he left there massacred and the settlement destroyed, Columbus established a forced labour policy among the natives, against the orders of the Queen. His attempt to rebuild the settlement and harvest gold for himself and the monarchy proved to be of little success and sparked hatred between the natives and the sailors. On July 31, 1498, Columbus "discovered" an island that was already inhabited by Amerindian peoples. This island was called "Land of the Humming Bird," by the natives and is presently known as the island of Trinidad.

The Amerindians' fight to keep the Europeans from colonising their island was unyielding and fiercely executed, but sadly it ended in failure. Between the war, enslavement and diseases, all experienced at the hands of the Europeans, the Amerindian population eventually dwindled from nearly 35,000 at the time of the European's arrival to roughly 300.

The descendants of these survivors presently live mainly on the Eastern side of the island. Columbus renamed the island la Trinidad and claimed it for Spain.

In 1783, a French planter named Roume de St. Lauren advised the Spanish King to issue a Cedula of Population, which was a plan designed to attract immigrants to the islands of Trinidad and Tobago with the promise of unrestrained land grants to any Roman Catholic citizen of any land loyal to Spain.

The population grew rapidly and comprised of mainly French planters with their slaves and free persons of colour flocking to the island to benefit from the Cedula.

CHAPTER TWO

THE IMPACT
OF SLAVERY

THE ATLANTIC SLAVE TRADE

The Atlantic slave trade, as the name suggests, was the voyage of slaves for trade across the Atlantic. It was also one of the most heart- wrenching, horrendous, life-altering events ever to happen in human history. Around 1650, as the development of plantations was on the rise, so too was the demand for slaves and during this period of human trafficking, an estimated 12 million Africans were viciously ripped from their homes and the lives they knew and forcibly sold.

The natives on the West Coast and other parts of Africa paid the ultimate price as they were captured through warfare or raids by other tribes and were traded to the European traders who bartered with the African traders using manufactured merchandise as payment for the trade of slaves.

Men, who were once strong and able bodied, were unable to defend themselves and their loved ones during the ordeal of being captured. Once used to the routine of their daily lives as carpenters, hunters or farmers, they were one day attacked and beaten without warning and dragged off in chains, confused, afraid and in excessive amounts of physical and emotional pain, worried about their future, their children, their wives, friends, siblings and parents.

Women were beaten and raped in front of their children and left helpless, bleeding and afraid of attacks from other tribes on their villages. Mothers watched in horror as their daughters were also raped, beaten and dragged away crying and fighting for their lives with all of their might. They longed for the nightmare to end and to be with their loved ones, but the nightmare never ended.

All that mothers could do throughout their ordeal was look on with a pain no one could comprehend as they watched their younger children being killed or crying out in pain as they were tortured and treated like animals.

Overwhelmed and scared children looked on in horror, unable to help themselves or their parents. The strong father who once corrected them with authority and who was shown such respect was now reduced to a weeping shell of a man, begging for the lives of himself and his family. In some cases, the father was killed and lay on the ground like trash, bleeding and battered. Their mothers were shamed in front of them, bleeding and hurt and their siblings were crying or dead.

All of the remaining victims were carried away in chains never to see each other again. Mothers were left wondering if the children were with the father, and the fathers wondered if the children were with the mothers. No one knew if the others were carried to the same location, if they were alive or dead or even where they were being taken.

Once traded to the Europeans, they were packed on ships like animals and faced far worse treatment and conditions than they could ever imagine possible. Their life as they knew it was no more and there was nothing they could do about it.

These newly captured and traded Africans were no longer viewed or treated as humans. In the eyes of their captors, they were just stock, like cattle and make no mistake, they were treated as such. Approximately 500 of them were packed into the hull of an overcrowded slave ship and compacted so densely there was not enough room to breathe properly.

The crew occupied the upper portion of the ship and seldom ventured into the holding area unless they were ordered to go and wash the slaves or to get a female to satisfy their sexual desires.

Apart from that, the crewmembers were usually afraid of their cargo, catching diseases and of the unknown, so they opted to stay away from the hull. A few buckets were placed in the hull of the ship for the slaves to use to relieve themselves. However, only the slaves closest to the buckets got the opportunity to use them as they were so closely packed and the tightly fitting shackles made walking through the crowded area not only difficult but dangerous to the slave. Therefore, some slaves opted to face the embarrassment and succumb to the yearnings of their bowels right where they stood or sat.

One can only imagine the different odours of urine, faeces, rotting flesh, blood, death and disease that amalgamated and erupted in the poorly ventilated, humid and hot area. Crewmembers, although unable to tolerate the stench, were sometimes ordered to go below and wash the slaves but for most of the voyage, filth covered the floors of the slave quarters.

On some of the ships, the slaves were fed twice daily as the traders needed healthy looking, strong, able-bodied stock to sell, for the better the stock the more money would be captured for them. On other ships, the slaves were seldom fed.

Many slaves, severely depressed about their situation, opted to commit suicide to escape their torture. Some would starve themselves to death in the hope that death would not only bring an end to their pain, but that they would find their way back to their homeland. Those who surrendered to death through this method would be used as examples by the crew who would cut the heads off the dead implying to the surviving slaves that they would either go back to their homeland headless or that they (the dead) could not find their way back to the homeland without a head. Other slaves who attempted to end their lives this way, had their mouths pried open and food force fed to them.

Other methods of suicide explored by the slaves were jumping overboard with the hope of drowning or being eaten by sharks or asking fellow slaves to strangle them. Whatever the method, suicide was the ultimate goal. Suicide was not the only way that death came to the slaves aboard ships, however.

Diseases such as smallpox and scurvy assisted with diminishing the slave population aboard the ship significantly along with the slaves who were murdered by the crew for different reasons, entertainment being one. There was little or no ventilation and infected wounds, unsanitary conditions and little or no space between the slaves was the perfect environment to incubate and spread diseases quite easily. Therefore, of the roughly 500 slaves aboard a vessel, nearly 100 would have died as a result of diseases both known and undiagnosed.

These conditions, along with the brutal treatment of the slaves lasted between 30 and 50 days on the seas with the slaves having no idea what was their fate, the fate of their families or what was next.

Clearly, we see that human trafficking started hundreds of years ago and was called the "slave trade."

THE SALE OF SLAVES

Having endured such a harrowing experience crossing the Atlantic aboard the slave ships and unaware of their fate, the slaves were then "prepared" for sale by the traders before being offloaded as the boats docked.

The stock of slaves was sorted and those with grey hair got it dyed black; the slaves had their skin oiled to have it appear healthy and to camouflage any skin defect and slaves with dysentery had corks inserted up their anus all in a bid to present a good stock of slaves for sale because the better-looking stock caught a higher price at the "scramble." The scramble was the name used at the height of the Atlantic Slave Trade to describe the earlier form of what was known as the slave auction.

The scared, crying, screaming, angry, feeble, sick, lonely and usually disheartened slaves were hustled into pens and surrounded by eager buyers as, they strong-armed and bulldozed each other in an attempt to position themselves rightfully to catch hold of the best stock when the starting gun was eventually fired. The scramble at times turned into a frenzy, resulting in fights among the purchasers. The buyers would then line up with their new possessions to both pay for them and to have the slaves branded with the initials of their owners.

This experience was just the first of many more horrors a slave would endure as it related to them being sold, because during a slave's life, they could be sold or traded several times. The sale or trading of slaves became known as a slave auction and it was widely publicised, drawing plantation owners from all over to witness the human merchandise up for sale.

The event was treated like an excursion as buses loaded with plantation owners and their families came to shop. Men, women, children, infants and entire families were placed on the auction block to be sold and this ultimately saw the division of families, unless they were purchased as a unit. The buyers inspected their intended purchases with no respect, and no consideration of the embarrassment experienced by the slaves was given. Slaves had their mouths pulled open and teeth examined. They were walked like dogs to detect lameness or any defect of the limbs; their bodies were searched for unnoticeable or disguised wounds and further to this already mortifying episode, they were bombarded with questions about their skills and experience.

The slaves were commanded to be cheerful and to put on a good show for the prospective buyers by their present owners who wanted top dollar for them and also their families and friends who wanted them to be sold as a unit to the same plantation. While waiting to be sold, some slaves would survey the sea of plantation owners and catch sight of a particular owner they preferred to be sold to. They would position themselves and act accordingly, discredit other slaves and promote themselves highly in a bid to be purchased by the preferred owner.

CHAPTER THREE

PLANTATION LIFE

THE PSYCHOLOGICAL IMPACT

A fter being separated, sold and sent to different plantations all over the world, life was never the same for the slaves. Different tribes were captured and sold to the traders, which meant a difference in languages, accents, beliefs and customs were now making communication between the slaves an extremely difficult task.

This barrier coupled with the fact that some of the tribes were probably banned from making contact with or mixing with neighbouring tribes, hindered communication among the slave population of the plantation. Nevertheless, despite the language barrier, the slaves bonded to some degree in their adversity and tried to manoeuvre through the new life forced upon them as best as they could. Plantations required both skilled and untrained labour to successfully run their businesses. Different countries and islands had different plantations that cultivated different crops such as sugar cane, salt ponds, rice, tobacco or cotton. Therefore, whichever plantation it was, skilled and unqualified workers were required to manage it effectively.

Skilled labourers were those Africans who were masons, joiners, blacksmiths, metal workers, nurses, seamstresses, etc and the unskilled workers were the ones who tended to the fields and animals.

Frederick Douglass' book "Narrative of the Life of Frederick Douglass", which was written in 1845, gives an insight into the conditions that slaves suffered at that time: *"There were no beds given the slaves, unless one coarse blanket be considered such, and none but the men and women had these... they find less difficulty from the want of beds, than from the want of time to sleep; for when their day's work in the field is done, the most of them having their washing, mending, and cooking to do, and having a few or none of the ordinary facilities for doing either of these, very many of their sleeping hours are consumed in preparing for the field work the coming day; and when this is done, old and young, male and female, married and single, drop down side by side, on one common bed—the cold, damp floor—each covering himself or herself with their miserable blankets; and here they sleep till they are summoned to the field by the driver's horn."*

There was no 8 am to 4 pm workday for the slaves on the plantations—There was only work until the slave overseer said to stop. Slaves were whipped for several reasons on the plantations, but one such reason would be to force them to work faster. However, lashes were not the only method implemented by the slave owners to get the slaves to work harder.

Some chosen slaves were given small incentives that varied from extra food or clothing to land for cultivating foodstuff and animals for their personal use. This simple act was a plan of the slave owner to manipulate said slaves into doing whatever the master wanted, be it to snitch on the other slaves or simply please the master.

The female slaves always fell prey to the deviant sexual habits of their owners, who took no notice of the slave's age, appearance or the fact that she was someone's wife or daughter and some of these slaves were impregnated during these shameful and degrading acts of rape.

House slaves were often the slaves with the lighter toned skin that lived and worked around the house of the slave owner. These were the "Mulatto" or "mixed persons" who came about by the mixing of the African or indigenous and European races when female slaves were taken advantage of and raped by their Caucasian male owners. And of course, this act represented the slave owner's ability to increase his slave stock without having to purchase more slaves as children born at the plantation were born into slavery and therefore, the "property" of the owner.

These mulattos were seen not just as a breeding unit, but also as an instrument to 'water down' or destroy this dark race by changing their unique complexion, hair texture, features, body structure and mindset. A female slave was embodied as property that a slave owner had full control over and therefore, the authority to take advantage of. These mulattos being beautiful "stock", were made house slaves, not just to serve their owners but to also "service" their male owners, create more slaves and have their beauty paraded among the owner's friends.

If you put considerable thought into this, life for a mulatto slave was anything but easier just because they were the preferred slaves. Preferred slaves for sex and breeding purposes were hated by the slave owners' wives as they were probably viewed as the object that took away the husband's attention and, in some cases, affection, and they were severely punished for this. Their offspring were inevitably viewed as better stock and taken away for the same purpose their mothers were being used.

Even if, in some rare instance, the father felt some type of compassion for his child born to a mulatto female slave, this child would never be granted freedom and would be mistreated by the wives of the slave master and her children. Although slaves disembarked the ship without family members in most instances, they eventually, over the years, started new families while on the plantations. Heartbreak and helplessness lay in their deck of cards as the owners at the same time owned every slave of the plantation and had the right to deal with his stock the way he wished.

Just as a farmer would walk into a pig pen or chicken coop and choose whichever animal, he desired to sell, trade or kill, so too did the slave owner exercise his right to choose any of his stock to sell, trade or kill. Therefore, even on the plantations new families were ripped apart as the members within a family were sold, traded or killed as examples to other slaves.

The one constant memory for the slaves was their African culture, customs and beliefs. Even though they may have varied from tribe to tribe, the features would have been similar enough for them to practice together. Memories of Africa strengthened and dominated the lives of the slaves.

Music and the practicing of their religious customs: Voodoo, Myalism and Obeah among others carried them through and gave them hope in traversing through their treacherous days at the plantation.

The slave owners, unable to understand these practices, were afraid of them and feared when the slaves gathered together to practice them. Thus, slaves were banned from practicing their customs and were forced to accept Christianity. This new religion was used as a powerful weapon against the slaves.

CHAPTER FOUR
THE IMPACT
ON AFRICA
A SOCIETY SHATTERED

A frica was never the same after the European slave traders came and bled the country of its highest, most valuable resource, its human resource. They left only a trail of orphaned children, as well as old, sick and diseased people to try to rebuild a nation, leaving the blind to lead the blind.

Africa, contrary to what we are led to believe, was a thriving nation, and a superior country filled with many resources. Africans from different states traded with each other and maintained a well-oiled society that catered to itself and needed no outside assistance or interference. From as early as the creation of the Egyptian Pyramids and the construction within the Roman city, we can ascertain that the people were versed in the fields of science, mathematics, art, technology and construction. The Yoruba people of Ife, as far back as 500 BC traded objects made from bronze, brass, copper, wood and ivory.

The Benin people were skilled in ivory carving, pottery, rope and gum production. West Africa was renowned for its gold, salt and copper collection and the Mali tribe traded gold dust and agricultural produce all throughout the West and Northeast regions of Africa, eventually, in the 14th century, relying on cowrie shells as currency.

African societies were coerced into the slave trade in the hope that it would be beneficial to them at some point. Nzinga Mbemba, ruler of the Kongo in the year 1491, after converting to Christianity and referring to the King of Portugal as his brother, fell victim to the Portuguese, who robbed him of his possessions and enslaved his people in exchange for rifles.

His "brother" the King of Portugal convinced him that the sale was necessary and useful. Understanding this will allow us to recognise the adverse impact the slave trade has had on Africa and understand its present state. Today the endeared Africa is a shell of its former self. Evident is the high level of flight of the continent's citizens as they have opted to gain all the knowledge, expertise, education and skills necessary to operate successfully in their respective fields and use these skills to gain employment elsewhere. Any other country will do, as they seek to leave Africa, allowing their society to remain vulnerable as they build the economy of another country. Evident also is the rise in wars, rebellion, colonialism, imperialism and tribalism among its people.

Ethnic fragmentation and the modification of populations to confine themselves to their respective boundaries have captured the continent as villages, tribes and states raid each other with the expectations of hostile retaliations. Religious wars such as the Morabout war and Toubenan Movement and tribal wars like those experienced between the Zulus and Pondos, Tutsi and Hutu and Ndebele and Shonda tribes have paved the way for the weakening of the African states, political instability, social disorder and the stagnation of the economic development.

PSYCHOLOGICAL IMPACT OF ABUSE

Abuse, be it physical, emotional/verbal, sexual or financial can be categorised as the unfair treatment of an entity for gain to the abuser. Although abuse itself may not cause psychological illnesses to occur, there can be an overpowering factor connecting abuse to certain disorders as victims commonly develop emotional or mental problems ancillary to their abuse.

The trauma or shock experienced by the victims of abuse may manifest under the form of anxiety disorders, depression, substance abuse disorders, posttraumatic stress disorder (PTSD), personality disorders, dissociative disorders, sexual disorders, suicidal tendencies, poor self-esteem and eating disorders.

For a victim of abuse, these disorders are difficult to heal from and in many cases bear a severely negative mental impact as the mind tries to process what has transpired. The victim's thought processes, emotions, feelings and behavioural patterns have been derailed, and therefore, stress has been placed their cognitive ability.

A study conducted by the American Psychological Association stated: "Given the prevalence of childhood psychological abuse and the severity of harm to young victims, it should be at the forefront of mental health." This shows that childhood psychological abuse changes the trajectory of a child's life and has far-reaching consequences that are damaging to the individual.

How then, looking back at slavery, could the slaves be expected to instil knowledge and proper direction to future generations when they themselves were in some cases irreversibly damaged. These slaves were conditioned to do, act and want what they were told to. They no longer had knowledge of what was right or wrong, as their previous belief of what was morally correct was met with violence and their captors rewarded actions that they knew to be erroneous. The moral compass that once directed their lives was now defective. It is no wonder why for generation after generation, the pain, hurt, mediocrity and self-hate have been passed on unknowingly.

It is no wonder that poor decision-making skills, and lack of empathy or emotions have been taught in a lesson to those who could have potentially been future leaders or why there is no longer a bond between families as fathers walk away from their responsibilities or disown their children in an uncaring, cold-hearted and sometimes ruthless manner.

This emotional numbness could have come forth from the slaves who refused to love another time after having their families ripped away and sold, raped or killed before their eyes as they looked on helplessly. Men had to mentally block the fact that their wives or daughters were being dragged off into the night by their owners to satisfy them or others sexually and then sent home to their husbands and fathers who were helpless to protect them.

Women became detached from their men as they were viewed as being undependable and worthless individuals who could do nothing to assist or protect them from the nightmare they endured and therefore no respect was given to their men folk.

Attachments were also withheld, as oftentimes the men would not return to them alive. It is, therefore, no wonder why some of our women see nothing wrong with sexually gratifying many partners in a bid to acquire material trinkets that they view as prestigious possessions.

More and more we see fewer women wanting to be married or wanting monogamous relationships. It is hardly surprising that there is a blatant lack of respect between the young and the old and even a more unconcealed insubordination for those in authority.

This stems from the young slaves having to witness in horror, helplessness, fear and disgust the most respected male slaves being castrated, beaten and buggered into submission and "broken in" like wild animals for all to see. These slaves, if they survived, would no longer be viewed with or command any respect from fellow slaves.

This lack of respect for authoritative male figures would have been passed on through the generations. If a woman is brutally raped, she will go through the healing process. However, if not properly counselled she will undoubtedly have many issues running rampant in the background of her mind that will inevitably display themselves in her thought patterns, behaviour and the upbringing of her offspring.

She may develop a fear of men, and this fear will inadvertently be passed on to her children. She may be angry all the time, not at her children but at herself, the perpetrator of the act and/or the situation that in her mind, ruined her life. From this anger, she may not ever be able truly to escape and it might be sometimes taken out on her children. She may suffer with depression, sleep disorders, eating disorders, low self-esteem and guilt, all of which becomes a normal way of life for her children. This is what is taught to them; this is what they learn, this is what they live and share with the next generation.

If we reasonably observe generations gone and present generations, we will discover that it is a complete race of misguided Africans making poor decisions and displaying handed-down issues, traits and disorders that were learned and therefore, exercised. We can also observe an entire Caucasian race of individuals, for many generations, exercising their perceived authority and superiority and proudly yielding it as a weapon against any race they see as inferior, regardless of their own status in life.

These are problems that stemmed from years of abuse developing into disorders that are not easy to combat and therefore, became corrupted teachings passed on from generation to generation.

THE ECONOMIC IMPACT

Slavery was a financially lucrative venture, as the labour was more or less free and the Portuguese and Dutch capitalised on this. The Dutch finance for investment helped others to turn the sugar production into a profitable business venture. Plantations in Barbados and St. Kitts tried many crops before settling on sugar production. In 1655, Jamaica joined in the production of sugar. Sugarcane was the dominating crop, and the demand for slaves was high because plantations grew, and the slaves were literally worked to death in the sugar fields.

Around the year 1750, an estimated 800,000 Africans had been imported into the Caribbean to work on the sugar plantations, yet the enslaved population was only 300,000. Even children as young as age five were put to work on the sugar plantations. By the year 1807, the annual income reported per estate was $4,000, which is equivalent to $400,000 in our present society.

More production meant more slaves, and that was equivalent to more money for the slave owners. Wealth for the slave owners was acquired literally off the backs of the slaves through their blood, sweat, tears and lives...just as it is today.

CHAPTER FIVE

THE HIDDEN HOLOCAUST

ATROCITIES AGAINST A PEOPLE

KING LEOPOLD II OF BELGIUM

From 1885-1908, King Leopold II was responsible for what his European coequals referred to as the "Congo Horrors." This was a name that perfectly described the level of cruelty faced by the natives of what was then called the Congo Free State but is known today as the Democratic Republic of the Congo.

Between 1891 and 1906, the private charitable organisation that collected rubber for export, and was operated by Leopold II could do whatever it wanted in that state with almost no judicial interference. Because of this freedom, the natives suffered drastically. There was forced labour and the hands of workers were cut off as punishment, Death or beatings came to those who refused to volunteer their services freely. Entire villages were destroyed and the Caucasian administrators such as Leon Rom, Leon Fievez (known as the "devil of Equateur") and Rene de Permentier, were free to indulge in their own sadism.

By the year 1901, an estimated 500,000 Congolese natives had died from sleeping sickness. Diseases such as smallpox, amoebic dysentery, venereal diseases and swine influenza that were imported by Arab traders, European colonists and African porters and famine ravaged these populations and killed more natives than the number killed by violence. This also explains the decline in the birth rate for this period and also explains the economic collapse of the Congolese people, their culture and their farming.

Sadly, because a native paramilitary army known as the Force Publique was created to enforce the labour policies, much of the violence committed against Africans in the Congo was by other Africans.

MENTAL CONDITIONING

The story has been told of the infamous Willy Lynch, slave owner in the West Indies in the year 1712, who documented and shared his method for controlling black slaves and guaranteed that if installed correctly, it would control slaves for at least 300 years. His method was the adoption of a combination of fear, distrust and envy for the purposes of control.

In his letter read on the bank of the James River in the colony of Virginia in the year 1712, he said: ***"Take this simple little list of differences and*** *think about them. On top of my list is "age", but it's there only because it starts with an "a". The second is "colour" or shade. There is intelligence, size, sex, sizes of plantations, status on plantations, attitude of owners, whether slaves live in the valley, or on a hill, East, West, North, South, have fine hair, coarse hair, or is tall or short.*

Now that you have a list of differences, I shall give you an outline of action, but before that, I shall assure you that distrust is stronger than trust and envy is stronger than adulation, respect or admiration. The black slaves after receiving this indoctrination shall carry on and will become self-refuelling and self-generating for hundreds of years, maybe thousands. Do not forget you must pitch the old black male vs the young black male, and the young black male against the old black male.

You must use the dark skin slaves vs the light skin slaves, and the light skin slaves vs the dark skin slaves. You must use the female vs the male and the male vs the female. You must also have white servants and overseers [who] distrust all blacks. But it is necessary that your slaves trust and depend on us. They must love, respect and trust only us. Gentlemen, these kits are your keys to control. Use them. Have your wives and children use them, never miss an opportunity. If used intensely for one year, the slaves themselves will remain perpetually distrustful"

Although it has been said that Willy Lynch never actually existed and the letter was nothing more than fiction and though the slave trade is no longer practiced today as it was centuries ago, mental conditioning is still being practiced to this day. The chains are hidden, but this dark-skinned race of people is still being beaten figuratively and poisoned to fight and hate each other.

EUGENICS

Another method of control was the implementation of a practice geared towards the improving of the genetic composition of the human population by a selective breeding program known as eugenics. Most people are aware of its practice by the Nazis, who labelled it the "Race Purification" project. It was more widely known as the Holocaust.

Author Jay Lifton wrote in his book titled "The Nazi Doctors—Medical Killing of the Psychology of Genocide(1986)", that Hitler had declared the sacred racial mission of the German people to be 'assembling and preserving the most valuable stock of basic racial elements[and]....Slowly and severely raising them to a dominant position.

However, years before Hitler embarked on this campaign, the concept was already being practiced to a large degree in the United States. In 1883 a British Scholar, Sir Francis Galton, first used the term "Eugenics" which meant "well-born" and believed the future of the human race could be directed by breeding individuals with "desired traits." This programme supported the forcible sterilisation of the poor, disabled and immoral simply because they believed that through selective breeding, the human species should direct its own evolution.

Of course, with the upper classes being predominantly Caucasian, it does not leave much to the imagination as to who the subjects of these experiments were. Michigan, in the year 1897, was the first U.S. state to introduce a compulsory sterilisation bill. It failed to get enough votes by legislators to be adopted, but eight years later Pennsylvania's state legislators passed a sterilisation bill.

Look around you and observe the laws that govern you. Ask yourself some difficult questions from time to time and if you do not know the answers, ask someone who does or do a little research. Ask questions like:

- Why is it that Caucasian men encourage their wives to stay at home and take care of the kids?
- Why are Caucasian women encouraged to make more children?
- Why are dark-skinned women being placed on birth control methods that are risky?
- Why are dark-skinned females told when to stop making babies?
- What are the results of prolonged use of the drugs associated with birth control?

LYNCHING

Lynching or vigilante justice was a way of life in the U.S. at one point. The act was named after Col. Charles Lynch as he and his associates made their own rules and exacted swift justice while manipulating the course of justice as it pertained to who he imagined criminal elements to be, by hanging the said perpetrators by the neck until they were dead.

Lynching, in the 1880's and onward openly displayed the repugnance and animosity felt by the Caucasian population towards the African population and any other ethnic group believed by the Caucasians to be inferior. The Ku Klux Klan is a movement in the U.S. that unabashedly advocates white supremacy, anti-immigration, white nationalism, Neo-fascism, Neo-Nazism, Anti-communism and the Christian Identity. This group set out as early as the 1860's to purify the American society of any group they opposed and utilised various methods to conduct their purification.

By the advent of the third manifestation of the Ku Klux Klan in the 1950s, their primary focus being the opposing of the Civil Rights Movement, there was a significant transformation in the tactics that the KKK employed toward achieving their goal. Violence and murder were some of the mechanisms commissioned by Klan members as they assiduously tried to control the African population.

The movement forged alliances with police departments and Governor's offices in places like Alabama to grapple with the works carried out by the Civil Rights Movement. They were also responsible for the beating, lynching, torturing, burning, bombing, chopping and ultimately the deaths of many Africans in America around that time.

Statistics have recorded that as early as 1882 to the year 1933, an estimated 3446 Africans met their demise through lynching. However, those were only the recorded cases as by the 1890's lynching was an activity used as a form of recreation, punishment and control and scores of Caucasian onlookers of all ages and genders were invited to what was touted as a rather jocund and entertaining event. Some of these events were advertised in the newspapers, and the macabre pictures were even generated into the form of postcards to be sent to persons who missed the event.

Body parts, including genitalia were barbarically cut from the bodies of the victims and kept as souvenirs. Some of the crimes punishable by lynching were:

- Incest
- Molestation
- Indolence
- Slander
- Running a bordello
- Inciting trouble
- Robbery
- Murder and attempted murder
- Fraud
- Pillage
- Voodooism
- Vagrancy
- Unruly remarks
- Demanding respect
- Making threats
- Arson inciting to riots
- Banditry
- Indolence
- Sedition
- Insulting a white man or woman
- Spreading diseases
- Slander

- Being obnoxious
- Informing
- Eloping with a white woman
- Trying to vote
- Injuring livestock

CHAPTER SIX

REBELLION AND REVOLUTION

A PEOPLE RISE UP

Frustration brought about by a life in chains oftentimes results in violence, and this is evident from past and present rebellions worldwide. Further evident, is the fact that when the Caucasian population fears the unifying of Africans, they put measures in place to ensure the day to day living conditions be unbearable in an attempt to humble the African masses.

This was discernible during and after slavery where both slaves and former slaves were met with harsher laws, oppressive legislation, harsher penalties for petty crimes, anti-abolitionist convictions etc. This has not changed much in this present day as we see mechanisms strategically put in place by the Caucasian population to suppress the African race. Groups of Africans congregating together are quickly dispersed and silent protests involving the coming together of a mass of Africans are often met with violence. Laws are regularly enforced unfairly based upon the race of the individual committing the crime, and oftentimes, the African offenders receive harsher punishments, disproportionate to the crime that was committed. The following is a list of slave rebellions that transpired between 1570 and 1832:

THE HAITIAN REVOLUTION

This was the most successful revolution in the history of slave rebellions. What started as a slave revolt ended with an independent state being granted to the slaves. In the year 1791, the slaves of the French colony of Santo Domingue organised a rebellion, which resulted in the death of thousands of Caucasians and saw the burning of sugar plantations.

The general of the slave army, Toussaint Louverture, continued his raging fight for three years until the French government officially abolished slavery in all its territories. After becoming governor of the island, Toussaint was captured during the year 1802 by Napoleon Bonaparte's imperial forces in a bid to reinstate slavery but the former slaves, having tasted the good flavour of freedom rejected this and again fought viciously to defeat the French forces.

On this occasion, led by Jean-Jacques Dessalines it took the slave army one year to defeat the French forces in what was named the Battle of Vertieres. The next year, the former slaves made a declaration of their independence and established the island as the Republic of Haiti.

BAPTIST WAR

Christmas Day in the year 1831 in the island of Jamaica will always be remembered for the massive general strike in which 60,000 out of 300,000 slaves, led by Baptist preacher and slave Samuel Sharpe, staged a peaceful protest. This quiet protest for basic amenities and a living wage ended in the death of over 600 slaves, burning and looting on the plantations for several days, $1.1 million in property damage and the death of 14 Caucasians in what was labelled the Baptist War. It was the largest slave uprising in British West Indies history, and even though it seemed unsuccessful the effects were felt across the Atlantic. A year later, slavery was abolished in the British Empire.

GASPAR YANGA'S REBELLION

Although this rebellion did not witness the death of slaves or Caucasians, nor the destruction of plantations, it did witness the establishment of the first official settlement of freed Africans in the Americas in 1630.

Having spent 40 years hiding in the forest after fleeing a sugar-cane plantation near Veracruz in the year 1570, Gaspar Yanga, an African slave, established a free settlement in Mexico which he and a small group of former slaves called San Lorenzo de los Negros.

Although authorities destroyed the colony in the year 1609, they were unable to capture Yanga's followers and eventually settled for a peace treaty with the former slaves. Yanga negotiated and was given the right to build his own free colony as long as taxes were paid to the Spanish Crown. This municipality still exists today as "Yanga."

NAT TURNER'S REBELLION

Nathanial Turner also called "Nat" was a slave who decided that being a slave would no longer benefit him or his future generations and effectively led a slave rebellion

in August 1831 in Virginia. Turner was a charismatic preacher who chose to lead the people out of bondage by striking fear throughout the Caucasian population in the South. On August 21st 1831, he and six other slaves killed the Trevis family, secured arms and horses and acquired the assistance of seventy-five other slaves.

During the insurrection, 51 Caucasians were killed and Turner paid the ultimate price as he was caught and hanged along with 16 of his followers. The fear instilled in the hearts of the white population propelled them to implement even harsher laws against the slaves and this all culminated in the Civil War.

CHAPTER SEVEN

BREAKING THE SHACKLES

THE JOURNEY BEGINS

On February 23, 1807, the British Parliament voted to abolish the slave trade. On March 25, 1807, the abolition of the Slave Trade Act was entered in the statute books. However, the trafficking of slaves between Caribbean islands continued until the year 1811.

The Bill stated that from January 1st 1808, it would be illegal to introduce into the United States, any "Negro," "mulatto'" or any person of colour, as a slave. The law also made provisions on the prohibition of any citizen financing or equipping a slave ship.

The penalties for same were:

1. A fine of $20,000.00, along with the loss of the ship for equipping a slave ship.

2. A fine of $5,000 along with the loss of the ship for the transporting of slaves

3. A fine of between $1,000 and $10,000, imprisonment of 5-10 years and forfeiture of both ship and slaves for carrying illegal slaves.

This should have been a joyous occasion for the slaves to witness a flicker of hope, which might bring an end to the turmoil and constant desolation of their people. It, however, was yet another unfulfilled dream as slaves were still in high demand, and human trafficking was a lucrative business. The hefty fines imposed for the illegal transport of slaves did not stop the callous tradesmen from continuing with the slave trade. It did, however, make the journey for the slaves doubly dangerous as the traders would prefer to lose the stock than pay the fines.

In one such instance, Captain Homans of the Brillante, having been surrounded by 4 British vessels trying to enforce the law of the ban on the trading of slaves, tied his 600 slaves to a huge anchor and drowned them at the bottom of the sea to eliminate the evidence and avoid prosecution. Today, in the Caribbean Sea off the Coast of Grenada, there is a monument created by Jason de Caires Taylors in honour of the slaves thrown overboard and those who were forced to jump while travelling through the Middle Passage from West Africa to the Americas of the Caribbean.

Slavery was finally abolished in the United States and the law was passed in Congress on January 31, 1865 and ratified on December 6, 1865. The 13th Amendment reads: "Neither slavery, nor involuntary servitude, except as a punishment for crime whereof the party shall have been duly convicted, shall exist within the United States, or any place subject to their jurisdiction."

CHAPTER EIGHT
OPPOSING THE SYSTEM
TURNING POINTS

Freedom from slavery was met with opposition and hurdles along the way, but it was something that the African ancestors fought for and won. For this and a host of other reasons, this race of humans can be proud of who they are.

However, the system that sought to keep Africans in subjection stayed in place, and to some extent remains to this day. Although over the years there have been many words used to describe the African/dark skinned race of people, one pillorying slang stands out—Jim Crow. Albeit a scoffing slang, it came to be known as any law passed in the South that had different rules for "blacks" and "whites." These "Jim Crow" laws were based on a theory of white supremacy where racism appealed to the Caucasian population who feared losing their jobs to the "blacks."

This was in a time where politicians abused the "blacks" to gain the votes of the "whites." In the 1890's the Jim Crow laws touched every part of life. Laws were enforced that segregated African and white textile workers and did not allow for them to work in the same room, pass through the same gates or gaze out the same windows. Many industries would not hire Africans and one was not permitted to marry outside of their race.

These laws witnessed Africans undergoing a curfew system and the discrimination of not being allowed to buy tickets from particular ticket booths nor being allowed to drink water from certain water fountains. Jim Crow laws were responsible for the segregation of schools, hospitals, prisons, colleges and even restrooms. There were separate textbooks for the different races, and books could not be stored together. In the courts, there were two Bibles for Africans and whites to swear on.

EMMETT TILL

Emmett Till was a 14-year-old boy who was visiting relatives in Money, Mississippi on the 24th day of August 1955 when he was wrongfully accused of whistling at a Caucasian female named Caroline Bryant at a grocery store and was brutally abducted and murdered.

Till, the only child of Louis and Mamie Till, was born on the 25th day of July 1941 in Chicago, Illinois. His father was a soldier who was executed while serving in Italy for "misconduct" and his mother who worked as a clerk responsible for confidential files in the Air Force, raised the young Till as a single mother.

Till was a responsible young man who didn't shy away from household chores, but assisted his mother by shouldering the workload at home, which included the laundry, cleaning and some cooking as she worked long hours to ensure that she and her son were well taken care of. Those who knew the child described him as responsible, funny and infectiously high spirited.

In August 1955, after spending time with family, Till's great uncle, Moses Wright, took him and a cousin to visit relatives in Mississippi. Although Mrs. Till was opposed to the idea and wanted to go to Nebraska instead, the young Till was excited to go with his great uncle and begged his mother to give him the permission he needed. It was on this ill-fated trip that he met his demise. Till and a group of teenagers ventured into Bryant's Grocery and Meat Market. After he purchased some bubble gum, it is unclear if he whistled, touched or flirted with the wife of the owner, Carolyn Bryant. Four days later, Carolyn's husband, Roy Bryant and his half-brother J.W. Milam, kidnapped Emmett from his great uncle's home and brutally beat the child, dragged him to the Tallahatchie River, shot him in the head, tied him with barbed wire to a large metal fan and shoved his body into the water.

Three days later, his corpse was pulled out of the river with the poor child's face mutilated beyond recognition. His uncle was only able to identify his body by a ring he wore, which bore his father's initials, L.T. Till's body was shipped back to Chicago where his mother made the painful decision to display his body for five days and have an open casket funeral so that the world would see what happened to her child.

Jesse Jackson, Baptist minister and Civil rights activist commented: "With his body water-soaked and defaced, most people would have kept the casket covered. [His mother] let the body be exposed. More than 100,000 people saw his body lying in that casket here in Chicago. That must have been at that time the largest civil rights demonstration in American history."

The trial following the burial of Till was completely biased, as no Africans were allowed on the all-male jury panel. Jet Magazine and The Chicago Defender printed the graphic pictures of the mutilated child and by September 1955, Till's death had sparked outrage throughout the nation. His uncle braved death by testifying against his nephew's murderers but despite the overwhelmingly solid evidence, Bryant and Milam were acquitted of all charges. Only a few months later, protected by double jeopardy laws, Bryant and Milam sold the story of how they killed Emmett Till to Look Magazine for $4,000. The death of Emmett Till was the main catalyst that fuelled the emergence of the Civil Rights Movement.

ROSA PARKS

Rosa Louise McCauley, known today as Rosa Parks, pioneer activist for Civil Rights was born on the 4th day of February 1913 in Tuskegee Alabama. She was no stranger to racial discrimination, as she was the granddaughter of two former slaves who were also proponents of racial equality.

Rosa did not achieve a higher level of education until she was married to Raymond Parks at the age of 19. She achieved her high school degree in the year 1933 and was thereafter actively involved in the Civil Rights movement, having joined the Montgomery chapter of the NAACP in 1943.

Mrs. Parks accrued some of the highest awards during her lifetime and even after her passing, she was still being honoured. Those awards included:

- The Spingarn Medal
- The Martin Luther King Jr. Award
- The Presidential Medal of Freedom
- The Congressional Gold Medal

After her passing at the age of 92, she was honoured with a U.S. Postal Service Stamp (Rosa Parks Forever stamp).

In 2009, a statue honouring her was unveiled by the then President Barack Obama. Rosa Parks will always be remembered for her act of bravery on that fateful day, December 1st 1955. Back then, the Montgomery City Code ensured that a bus driver was given the power to assign seats to the passengers as all public transportation was segregated. This meant that a line was drawn across the middle of the bus and beyond the line, to the back of the bus, was the seating area for Africans and the front of the bus accommodated Caucasians.

However, there were instances where the front seats were filled, and the bus driver would require the first few seats beyond the white line to be made available to the Caucasian passengers. On the day in question, Rosa Parks and three other

Africans were required to give up their seats for the driver to make his Caucasian passengers comfortable. Parks was the only one who did not comply and she was subsequently arrested. She said she was tired of giving in, and that was her reason for not satisfying the request of the bus driver.

That very evening, E.D. Nixon, head of the local chapter of the NAACP, outraged by the arrest of Parks, organised a boycott of Montgomery City Buses, and used the opportunity to create change. The message of the planned bus boycott was sent out secretly. On the 5th of December 1955, people were encouraged to stay at home, take a cab or walk to work if remaining at home was not an option.

That day was also the day scheduled for Rosa Parks' trial. The support for Rosa was overwhelming as 500 supporters greeted her in front of the courthouse as she arrived with her attorney. She was found guilty of violating a local ordinance and was fined $10 as well as a $4 court fee.

Although a seemingly insignificant act, Rosa's actions triggered one of the biggest and most successful events in the Civil Rights Movement. This Montgomery bus boycott saw an estimated 40,000 commuters opting to walk to work, with some walking as far as 20 miles. The boycott went on for several months and acutely paralysed the bus company's finances. This was met with the strong and intemperate retaliation of the segregationists. They took reprisals by bombing the homes of both Martin Luther King Jr. and E.D. Nixon, burning African owned churches, cancelling the insurance on African-owned taxis and arresting citizens for the infringement of an antiquated law prohibiting boycotts.

An all-African legal team represented the members of the community and in June 1956, the Jim Crow segregation laws were proclaimed to be unconstitutional by the district court. The decision was appealed, but on November 13, the U.S. Supreme Court declared that the ruling of the lower court would be ratified.

CHAPTER NINE
THE BLACK MARTYRS
MAKING THE ULTIMATE SACRIFICE

MEDGAR EVERS

Medgar Evers, an educated and accomplished husband and father of three beautiful children, fought feverishly against discrimination from as early as 1952 until his untimely death on June 12, 1963 at the age of 38. He became involved in the Regional Council of Negro Leadership, spearheading a boycott against gas stations that refused to allow Africans to use their public restrooms. He then worked on behalf of the National Association for the Advancement of Coloured People and volunteered with the NAACP, thereafter becoming their secretary.

Mr. Evers recruited new members for the NAACP and organised voter-registration efforts. He led demonstrations and economic boycotts of "white" owned companies that practiced discrimination. Mr. Evers also fought against racial injustice and was instrumental in reforming laws related to crimes against African Americans. One such crime was against Emmett Till.

In May 1954, the U.S. Supreme Court handed its decision in the Brown vs. Board of Education case where the segregation of schools came to an end. This was another battle where Evers made a significant contribution. Evers was the most prominent civil rights activist in Mississippi until his death on June 12, 1963.

Because of his notoriety, he was targeted by people who were averse to racial equality and desegregation. Multiple threats and acts of violence were levied on Mr. Evers and his family. Their home was firebombed in May of 1963 and finally Evers was shot and killed in the driveway of his home on June 12, 1963.

Almost 31 years after his passing, several appeals and three trials later, Byron De La Beckwith, a white segregationist and the founder of the Mississippi White Citizens Council were beyond recall, convicted and sentenced to life in prison for Evers' murder.

Evers' works are perpetuated by his wife and brother and great strides were made because of the sturdy foundation he laid. His contributions to the civil right movement were appreciated and honoured with the U.S. Navy entrusting his name to one of their vessels, a Campus in the City University of New York being named after him and his wife continuing the couple's commitment to change by creating the Medgar and Myrlie Evers Institute in Jackson Mississippi.

MARTIN LUTHER KING

Martin Luther King Jr., a visionary leader committed to attaining social justice through non-violence, experienced his fair share of criticism and lack of support from the very people he was dedicated to assisting.

King, born Michael King Jr. on January 15, 1929 to Michael King Sr. and Alberta Williams-King in Georgia was a happy middle child. His father, in a bid to pay homage to a German Protestant religious leader named Martin Luther changed his own name to Martin Luther King Sr. and Michael Jr. followed in his father's footsteps, adopting the name, and became known as Martin Luther King Jr.

Although Martin Luther King Jr. became revered and respected as the man who made significant reform where race relations was concerned, his peaceable and unwarlike approach to handling these matters was condemned by many. King was nurtured in a devout and disciplined home where both his father and grandfather were renowned religious leaders. He was a bright and determined student and was awarded his degree in the year 1955.

He later married Coretta Scott and had four wonderful children and later became pastor of the Dexter Avenue Baptist Church of Montgomery Atlanta.

Martin Luther King Jr. was instrumental in changing several laws to the benefit of the individuals he was dedicated to fighting for. Some of these include:

- The lifting of the law mandating segregated public transportation.
- The registering of black voters and ultimately the passage of the Voting Rights Act of 1965
- The ending of segregation at lunch counters
- The passage of the Civil Rights Act of 1964 authorising the Federal Government to enforce desegregation of public accommodations and outlawing discrimination in publicly owned facilities.

However, as valiantly as he crusaded, his efforts were met with much criticism and opposition by fellow activists and supporters alike as his methods were deemed non-effective, weak and passive.

But even his method of non-violence was dangerous in itself, as in many instances, protestors were attacked by the police with night sticks, dogs, tear gas, etc. with many people being severely injured.

One such peaceful protest on the 7th of March 1965 was dubbed "bloody Sunday" as it described perfectly what transpired on that fateful day. King's methods of protest were well calculated and executed to minimise human injury while achieving his objectives. He admitted on the heels of being incarcerated in the spring of 1963 that "non-violent direct action seeks to create such a crisis and foster such tension that a community, which has constantly refused to negotiate is forced to confront the issue."

King opened the eyes of the people, both Africans and Caucasians and allowed them to question laws and behaviour that were directed to the African population. This eye-opening experience helped Africans to realise that they themselves were standing in the way of their freedom and that the day of ending their subjection at the hands of another was, in fact, a reality. But they needed to stand for something and stop ignoring and taking for granted what their situation was and change it instead.

CHAPTER TEN
BLACK ACHIEVEMENTS
AFRICAN INNOVATION AND INVENTION

P resently, even though not widely known, there are inventions that are used daily in our society that were invented by a fellow dark skinned African. The following is a list of the contributions made as notable inventors and inventions that this race can be proud of:

- Air conditioning invented by Frederick Jones in 1949
- Almanac invented by Benjamin Banneker in 1791
- Auto cut-off switch invented by Granville Woods in 1839
- Auto fishing device invented by George Cook in 1899

- Baby buggy invented by William Richardson in 1889
- Biscuit cutter invented by Alexander Ashbourne in 1875
- Blood bag invented by Charles Drew in 1945
- Chamber commode invented by Thomas Elkins in 1897
- Clothes dryer invented by George Sampson in 1971
- Closed circuit TV invented by Marie Brown in 1966
- Curtain rod invented by Samuel Scrottron in1892
- Curtain rod support invented by William Grant in 1896
- Dooknob invented by Osbourn Dorsey in 1878
- Door stop invented by Osbourn Dorsey in 1878
- Egg beater invented by Willie Johnson in 1884
- Electric lamp bulb invented by Lewis Latimer in 1882
- Elevator invented by Alexander Miles in 1867
- Eye protector invented by Powell Johnson in 1880
- Fire escape ladder invented by Joseph Winters in 1878
- Fire extinguisher invented by Thomas Marshall in 1872
- Folding bed invented by Lenard Bailey in 1899
- Folding chair invented by Nathaniel Alexander in 1911
- Fountain pen invented by Walter Purvis in 1890

- Furniture caster invented by David Fisher in 1878
- Gas mask invented by Garrett Morgan in 1914
- Golf tee invented by George Grant in 1899
- Guitar invented by Robert Fleming Jr. in 1886
- Hairbrush invented by Lydia Newman in 1898
- Hand stamp invented by Walter Purvis in 1883
- Ice cream scoop invented by Alfred Cralle in 1897
- Insect destroyer gun invented by Albert Richardson in 1899
- Ironing board invented by Sarah Boone in 1887
- Keychain invented by Frederick Loudin in 1894
- Lantern invented by Michael Harvey in 1884
- Lawn sprinkler invented by John Smith in 1899
- Lemon squeezer invented by John Thomas White in 1893
- Lock invented by Washington Martin in 1893
- Lunch pail invented by James Robinson in 1895
- Laser surgical device (Laserphaco Probe) invented by Patricia Bath in 1986
- Mailbox invented by Paul Downing in 1891
- Mop invented by Thomas
- Stewart in 1893
- Peanut butter invented by George Carver in 1896
- Pencil sharpener invented by John Love in 1897
- Record player arm invented by Joseph Dickinson in 1819
- Refrigerated trucks invented by Frederick McKinley Jones in 1939

- Rolling pin invented by John Reed in 1864
- Shampoo headrest invented by Charles Bailiff in 1898
- Spark plug invented by Edmond Berger in 1839
- Stethoscope invented by Thomas Carrington in 1876
- Straightening comb invented by Madam C.J. Walker in 1905
- Street sweeper invented by Charles Brooks in 1890
- Phone transmitter invented by Granville Woods in 1884
- Thermostat control invented by Frederick Jones in 1960
- Traffic lights invented by Garrett Morgan in 1923.
- World's fastest computer invented by Philip Emeagwali in 1954

More to be proud of is the fact that even in the field of science, contributions were made by members of this beautiful race of people. The following is a list of renowned scientists:

- Professor Lewis Grant is a leading microbiologist and pathologist affiliated with the University of the West Indies, Mona (Jamaica)
- Dr. Marcia Roye is a biochemist who earned her PhD in Biochemistry from the University of the West Indies.
- Dr. Shirley Jackson is a physicist who received her PhD from the Massachusetts Institute of Technology.

- Benjamin Banneker was an astronomer and mathematician
- Charles Drew was a physician and surgeon
- Ernest Everett Just was a biologist
- George Washington Carver was a scientist
- Mae Jemison was a physician and astronaut and the first African woman to travel to space
- Marie Maynard Daly was the first female member of this amazing race of people to earn a PhD in chemistry
- Norbert Rillieux was an engineer
- Patricia Bath was an ophthalmologist
- Prof. Samuel Massie Jr. was an organic chemist.

Great strides were also made in the line of sports and the following is a list of athletes that we can all be proud of:

- Muhammad Ali is the undisputed greatest of all time in the field of boxing
- Jackie Robinson was inducted into the Hall of Fame in 1962 after being the first African baseball player
- Mabel Fairbanks was the first African figure skater and was inducted into the U.S. Figure Skating Hall of Fame.
- Mike Tyson was a boxing champion
- Carl Lewis represented as an athlete in track and field
- Dwight Yorke a talented soccer player from Trinidad and Tobago was nicknamed "the Smiling Assassin"
- Boxer Emile Griffith of the Virgin Islands
- Serena Williams

- Cullen Jones
- Earvin "Magic" Johnson
- Florence Griffith Joyner
- Michael Jordan represented in the field of basketball and was referred to as "Air Jordan"
- Merlene Ottey of Jamaica represented as a track and field athlete
- Sir Vivian Richards was referred to as the "Master Blaster" as he took the sport of cricket to new heights
- Brian Lara, hailing from Trinidad and Tobago is arguably the most entertaining cricketer of all time and may never be matched with skill.
- Sir Garfield Sobers is known to be the best all round cricketer in history
- Usain Bolt from Jamaica seems to have the fastest feet in the world.
- Cynthia Cooper was a basketball powerhouse and Olympic gold medal recipient
- Dominique Dawes is an Olympic medal winner in the field of gymnastics
- Carl Lewis won nine Olympic gold medals in Track and Field
- Arthur Ashe represented in the field of tennis

These are just a few people we can emulate and find great satisfaction and pride in the results of their accomplishments. In some cases, these persons were the "hidden figures" as their achievements and contributions stood out even though they were unknown. Much like the scientific contributions of Katherine Johnson, Mary Jackson and Dorothy Vaughan to NASA's mission in a time where segregation and the social disparities were prevalent.

CHAPTER ELEVEN

CHAINS OF MENTAL SLAVERY

THE REMNANTS OF BONDAGE

W hy is it that this dark-skinned race of people is the sole race that appears to be so curious about every other race, resulting in them unintentionally hating themselves and the way they look?

The women who were ridiculed during slavery and paraded like circus freaks because of their body structure and well-rounded derriere were made to believe that it was their lone asset and were made to feel inferior because of it.

Now, we can look at photos online, billboard advertisements and music videos and be bombarded with all shapes and sizes of dark-skinned derriere. Why? Is it that years later, we believe that this truly is our only asset?

This dark race is the only race of people desperately trying to fit in with the crowd and who are willing to do whatever it takes to accomplish same, even at the risk of putting themselves and their future generations in harm's way. They spend thousands of dollars trying to change their features, the very features that make them unique, like their hair, nose, cheekbones and complexion, in an attempt to look more like another race.

However, make no mistake, even though a woman of another race may undergo surgery to increase the size of her derriere, she is in no way trying to become "black" nor does she want to be associated with the stigma of being "black." Perhaps the action of securing a bigger, well rounded derriere is laced with jealousy at the amount of attention the dark-skinned female gets with having such an "asset."

In countries like Jamaica, Nigeria, Columbia and in the Caribbean, big butts have been a desirable asset on a female for centuries. In the UK, there was a 13% rise in fat transfer operations where fat was taken from the stomach or thigh area and squeezed into the buttocks according to Vice UK. When interviewed, some women indicated that they did butt lifts or fat transfer operations because they wanted to feel and look good as they would have a more accepted feminine look.

We speak of many years of slavery and don't realise that mental chains still hold many people captive even today. So much so, that our dark-skinned males make up most of the prison population in some countries around the world. After analysing statistics of incarcerations conducted in 2009 in the United States, 65% of all inmates were African Americans. Of 2.2 million male inmates, 67% of those were African

Americans as of 2014 (U.S. Department of Justice, 2014).

According to the National Association for the Advancement of Colored People (NAACP), African Americans constitute virtually 1 million of the 2.3 million incarcerated population, and have nearly six times the incarceration rate of whites. The remaining 1.3 million prison inmate population is made up of a mixture of races.

Let's look a little deeper and formulate a judgment based upon the information revealed. In some companies, you will see the "face" of the company being a woman of African descent with a lighter toned skin. Nowadays, everyone wants to be "mixed" or "white," and no one seems to be proud of their "darkness" anymore and the sad thing is, no other race wants to look like them. This seems to be years of conditioning of the mind at work where the "here and now" is the only priority and no thought about the future or of the possible effects it may have, is even considered.

Perhaps, arguably, selfish is an appropriate word to describe such individuals. During slavery, the slaves outnumbered the Caucasian slave owners significantly and this was a frightening reality for the slave owners. Consider for a moment what would happen if all the slaves, who outnumbered the Caucasian slave owners decided to revolt. Therefore, mechanisms had to be formulated and executed to control the slave population. Although many methods were used to dominate the slaves and keep them in subjection, one effective method where the consequences are still evident today was mental conditioning. They put slaves against each other. House slaves versus field slaves, I am better than you slave.

MODERN-DAY SLAVERY

Some argue that we are free, and that slavery was abolished, but look around and watch all the new millennium slaves still shackled to their masters. Sadly, slavery exists today and goes unnoticed by many who refuse to admit its existence. Be it the movie or music industry, clothes and brand-name sneakers or a certain lifestyle, slavery is the system in which individuals are owned by others who control their lives. Slavery exists today in different forms.

CHILD LABOUR

Children in the western part of Africa are plagued by intense poverty and begin work at a very young age in order to support their families. Some of these children are sold to work on farms, and others are abducted. These children are required to work long hours under terrible work conditions for as little as $2.00 per day.

THE CHOCOLATE INDUSTRY

Chocolate is the product of cocoa beans and is widely supplied by Ghana and the Ivory Coast which accounts for approximately 70% of the world's cocoa. These cocoa farms in Western Africa have been recently exposed as using child labour and some cases slavery. The ages of the children working on these farms are between 12 and 16.

There have also been reports of children as young as 5 years old working on these farms. These children are sold to the farms, in some instances by their parents who need the money and are assured the child will be well taken care of. Others are orphans who were told they would have a better life. Finally, there are those who were abducted and forced to work on the farms until they are old.

CHILD SOLDIERS

Vulnerable children, because of their age and physical and emotional immaturity, are targeted for military recruitment. According to the Human Rights Watch, these children are poor, separated from their families, displaced from their homes, living in combat zones or have limited access to education. These children, both girls and boys, are recruited forcibly in some instances or are disillusioned with the promise of food.

HUMAN TRAFFICKING

According to the UNODC—United Nations Office on Drugs and Crime, based on data gathered from 155 countries, 79% of human trafficking is for sexual exploitation, with the victims being predominantly women and girls. Approximately 30% of the countries provided the gender of traffickers, and surprisingly women make up the largest number. Women are selling women into slavery. Around 18% of human trafficking is forced labour. In parts of Africa children make up 100% of trafficking victims and worldwide, children make up 20% of human trafficking victims.

SEX TRAFFICKING

This is a form of slavery that exists globally. Traffickers use tactics such as violence, lies, threats and debt bondage to coerce children and adults into the sex trade. Vulnerable populations are targeted such as homeless persons, runaways, war victims, physically abused persons or societal outcasts.

These are just a few examples of slavery existing in these modern times. Imagine if the present-day "slaves" decided to open their eyes and recognise that they outnumbered their captors. What chaos would transpire?

MENTAL SLAVERY

The "house slaves vs field slaves" mentality is what is exhibited today, and yet we do not view these actions as those installed in us since the days of slavery. Colour consciousness is one such mentality exhibited by many people today, which often goes unnoticed and discarded as a normal reaction that can be explained and therefore, justified. We hear things like "black and ugly" when describing persons of a darker complexion. Why is it that ugly is associated with being black? Mental conditioning perhaps?

We hear things like: "The mother and father are dark in complexion, but if you see the fair nice baby they had" or: "If I was a little fairer, I would be prettier and happy" or you might hear two dark-skinned people arguing over who has softer hair. or fairer skin. We see our beautiful dark-skinned females bleaching and damaging their skin in an attempt to look fairer. If these are not examples of mental conditioning at work, then what is?

When the word psychonegrosis first came to my attention, I honestly thought someone was playing around with another word to embarrass this dark race of people, but to my surprise when I checked its definition, I was astonished.

According to Dr. Rick Wallace, Ph.D in an editorial dated the 29th day of August 2015, psychonegrosis is the mental psychosis that blocks black progression. Psychonegrosis is defined as a mental disorder affecting the spirit, personality, motives and actions of Negroes who have failed to rid themselves of the psychological ills they have accrued from their collective experience with foreigners. It is marked by a distorted ideal of self and others.

Psychonegrosis results in unnatural patterns of perception, logic, thought, speech, behaviour and emotional expression and is accompanied by various other unnatural dispositive manifestations (such as but not limited to self-group depreciation, the championing of non-black ideas, conversion to non-black religions, xenophilia, especially Anglo-centric xenophilia, cognitive dissonance, sexual deviation, escapism, dual or double consciousness, conflicting loyalties, and unscrupulous liberalism)—differing in degrees of severity from one individual to another. Psychonegrosis causes black people to be unreasonable, contradictory and utterly dependent upon (or considerate of) the culture, products, charity and sympathy and or conscience of other peoples, especially of white peoples.

CHAPTER TWELVE

THE CHANGE

CREATING A SENSE OF URGENCY

How many times have you seen a dark-skinned person of another nationality speaking with an accent or in a different language and wondered to yourself: "Why doesn't he/she go back to their country?" You may have gone for a job interview and perhaps another dark-skinned person of another nationality gets the job ahead of or instead of you, and you decide to sabotage them?

How many people have made sure that their loud, overbearing dark-skinned neighbour who is of another nationality gets evicted or even deported? In their mind, they justify their actions by reasoning that this person is a foreigner in their land, eating the food meant for their enjoyment, enjoying the pleasures designed for their fellow countrymen and acquiring the limited jobs which should be available only to them and theirs.

Secretly, they know that these actions are not acceptable as it conflicts significantly with their moral and ethical teachings. However, because of cognitive dissonance, they still commit the act. This self-justification makes the negative outcome more tolerable and is elicited as hedonistic dissonance. There are instances where blame is directed to the other person and the perpetrator refuses to embosom any of the responsibility. It's not hard to see how the Africans could have sold the Israelites and other tribes into slavery now that we understand how dissonance could have affected the way they reasoned the situation. It certainly does not make their actions ethical; it was and will always be an inhumane act to sell another human into slavery and that, is an undeniable fact. However, we can now understand to some degree, how it was done and how assume could find comfort in their actions after perpetrating this heinous act.

This dark race of people, in my opinion, has been disillusioned for so long, ignorant of who they really are and have been referred to by so many names that they are confounded as to what to call themselves. They have been called niggers, negroes, house niggers, coloured, creole, mulatto, quadroon, octoroon, African Americans and even blacks.

I am sure most of us went to school and learned about different colours on the colour charts. So, with that being said, it is quite evident that even the darkest man or woman is still just dark brown in complexion.

Arguably, this word "black" is now and has always been another terminology devised and introduced by the Caucasian population as a derogatory, disparaging and belittling word.

We also need to understand that not even "white people" are white, but they associate the colour white with purity and black with negativity and gloom. Therefore, your confessions are actually sending positivity their way and negativity in your direction. The word "black" has over the years been associated with many negative perceptions and ideas. For example, one is cautioned to wear white to weddings and black to funerals. Coincidental? I think not. There are also terms such as black magic, black spot, black sheep, black cat, black Friday, blacklisted and black widow, all designed to instil fear and discharge negative connotations.

Married with the knowledge of the power of confessions, does one still think it acceptable to refer to a nation of people as "black"? Today we have "Black" on black crime; "Black" homes without fathers; "Black" people on drugs; "Black" people going through severe poverty; "Black" women bleaching their skin to look white; No togetherness among "black" communities; "Black" people not liking themselves and doing face/body alterations; "Black" people being #1 in negative effects across the board; "Black" people being #1 in HIV and diabetes; "Black" people refusing to love their natural hair.

Oftentimes, dark-skinned persons go shouting to the hills "I am proud to be black," but would they really be proud of being black, if they knew the genesis of the word black to identify a people? If the word "black" was designed to tear down a nation of people and denigrate their existence, then how can you be proud to be such?

Perhaps you should consider being proud to be human, alive, healthy, happy, married, able to live a comfortable life, educated or in a home where both parents reside. We see our brothers greeting each other with the slang "my nigger." How did we reach to the point where we have embraced and accepted the hurt and pains associated with these types of words to the extent where we dispense it, and the negativity associated with its use as a daily greeting? We see our sisters referring to their friends and foes as "bitch." The last time I checked, this was the term used to refer to a female dog. Perhaps we should utilise more powerful words to build and not tear down our friends. "Hey beautiful" sounds considerably more acceptable than "hey bitch."

Because of this, I ask myself sometimes, to whom do black lives really matter? It seems evident to me that it does not matter to us (the dark community) unless conveniently. We are guilty of mistreating each other and yet rally around a "fallen brother" when he is mistreated by a person of the Caucasian race. So convenient! But we still see our brothers selling each other drugs or guns, killing each other like animals, pimping our sisters or passing each other on the streets like strangers without so much as a "hello."

Why is it that we must always greet or be introduced as "my black brother" or "my black sister"? I have not seen or heard anyone introduce a Korean, Caucasian or Vietnamese brother or sister by first referring to his or her complexion or race. Even if the person one is being introduced to is blind, I cannot fathom why one needs to identify race. This is a negative form of mental conditioning at work. Are you the introducer, secretly telling the person to hold on to their purses or pockets, or perhaps you are consciously trying to convince yourself that you can see past skin colour and race?

Every time we call ourselves black, we are speaking something negative into our lives and the generations following. It simply means that we are criticising and suppressing a people and as it is known, the power of confessions is a powerful thing, be it positive or negative. You are dark-skinned, and this darkness ranges through different hues, so being proud about this is important to your development. This dark skin is melanin rich and melanin protects against the effects of ultraviolet radiation; it neutralises the harmful effects of other dangerous types of radiation. It causes the skin to remain younger looking, and it aids in human reproduction. This is something to be proud of.

FORMING A POWERFUL COALITION

Africans should no longer try to be socially compatible, invisible or blend into the system but should aspire to transfigure or modify the system completely. When this is realised then one can agree that the consciousness of the people has been liberated. The cycle of bad choices and misguided teachings is what plagues our society from generation to generation. Unless identified and changed it will continue to plague, disable future generations and form a degenerative cycle.

We are obligated to understand what needs to be addressed before changes are made. Unjust and prejudicial treatment of all levels in every society is something that dark-skinned people, as a whole, face daily around the world. However, understanding and appreciating the worth or merit of a dark-skinned man or a dark-skinned woman will motivate us to do better and ignore the efforts to paralyse the growth of this race of people.

I was once told by an old woman "no one pelts the unready fruit" and as I analysed her words, I realised that this saying could be used to remedy many mentally disturbing situations that we may face. Put simply, no one tries to keep you immobile if you are not mobile, but the moment you try to become mobile, obstacles will be placed before you to hinder your mobility. When a person is ready to be promoted or make significant improvement to their lives, they get the most opposition or disappointment. This is not only geared towards demotivating persons, but it assists in keeping dark-skinned people in a mediocre mental state where their goals and dreams are inhibited and/ or limited to what they think is practical because they are conditioned not to want too much or aim too high.

Black consciousness is more than a movement of the 1960's after the Civil Rights movement of the 1950's, it's more than knowing your history, and it is not just a means to an end. Black consciousness allows dark-skinned people to embrace who they really are and cultivates pride in their identity. It allows us to understand that we are not just appendages to the Caucasian population. It empowers and propels the dark-skinned society to want and do more and not be ashamed or apologetic about who they and what they can accomplish.

Present-day rebellions need not to be with guns and knives. We can embark on a mental war that would definitely bring about change in this dark race and the way we view ourselves. We are by far a brilliant race, a creative people, resilient and strong both physically and mentally. We have built the empires that other races enjoy and benefit from, and we have invented things that others can only dare to dream about. Our athletic abilities are of world-class standard and we as a people can synthesise and build an empire for ourselves that is so well reinforced it can neither be infiltrated nor collapse.

The time has come for us to use our minds in this new millennium revolution. We need to rise above the hatred, teach our children how to be leaders and own companies, teach them how to become successful businessmen, purchase from each other and let the money circulate among the African community, build and support African schools, doctors, professionals and hospitals.

Let's stop selling guns and drugs to African brothers and sisters. Let's stop entertaining the illegal requests of the other races who cannot and would not execute those requests themselves. Let's grow our own food and love and respect each other.

These simple acts would be effective in achieving four things:

1. Healing the hurt of the African race.

2. Affecting the pockets of the other races and allow the tables to turn for the African race to finally have the respect it deserves.

3. Breaking the shackles.

4. Creating a unified consciousness among the African community

CHAPTER THIRTEEN
A VISION FOR CHANGE
CONSCIOUSNESS OF THE MIND

T he greatest fear of the "white" population is having the "black" population become united, knowledgeable and empowered. The late William James (1842-1910), an American philosopher and psychologist, once said: "We know the meaning of "consciousness" so long as no one asks us to define it.

How correct he was, as many persons do not understand fully, nor can they explain the meaning of the word consciousness. Basically, the term refers to the awareness of an individual to their thoughts. This includes sensations, their emotions and their memories. It is a stream of thoughts separate from each other that follows smoothly after each other and combines to give a unified consciousness even though consciousness is always changing.

Have you ever noticed that while watching a show on television, for example, a particular part of the show takes you back to a memory or an experience? You may start thinking about a task you have to accomplish later in the day, or you contemplate something you neglected to accomplish yesterday, all while your eyes are still focused on the show. Although your stream of consciousness might have been disturbed a few times during the show, it is amazing how you could still understand and enjoy the show. Your initial goal to watch the movie was accomplished even though at times you were distracted and this constant change of consciousness was taken for granted. So too, should the consciousness of the dark-skinned people be ever evolving. The consciousness of this body of people should coalesce and amalgamate to form a unifying force, a unified consciousness, an unbroken stream.

Consider something as small as an ant. One ant may go unnoticed and can cause no major harm or destruction, but a colony of ants will cause panic. Their bond and togetherness consolidate in helping them to accomplish their task. When one ant is killed the others do not decamp but tighten the formation and persevere until the task is completed. This is an example of procuring one stream of consciousness.

This dark race can take an example from nature. Positive change, although sometimes it is not fully accepted or appears difficult to receive, is a good thing. In order for us to throw off our negative attitudes and behaviours, we first need to establish what those negative attributes are. In other words, one needs to accept the fact that they are not perfect, and that they do indeed possess these negative attributes.

Obviously, nobody is perfect and no matter how much we may try to maintain a perfectly positive outlook in life, there is always some negativity looming in the shadows. The goal should be, however, to minimise the amount of negative thoughts, and try as much as possible to focus on the positive. Then, one must want to eradicate these negative traits and finally develop positive mental mechanisms to extinguish said traits.

Understanding that we assimilate both negative and positive attributes is the first step in ushering in the necessary change we want. Of course, changes won't be as meteoric as we might like. Changing a way of thinking is one of the most difficult things to do, because as the saying goes, old habits are hard to break. But once an individual can identify the changes to be made, however, then one can now possess some measure of control, gradually changing their mindset and thereby allowing balance to take hold.

As simple as this may sound, the magnitude of power you will gain by changing your mindset will allow you the individual to chart a new course for yourself. It means that neither the negative nor the positive attributes have the power to hold you captive and you can now make the choices that are beneficial to you.

The following questionnaire will help you establish what negative attributes you possess:

Question	Yes	No
Do I think I am always right?		
Do I get angry when corrected?		
Do I exercise peace and love?		
Do I place money ahead of my loved ones?		
Am I a selfish person?		
Is it hard for me to give of myself?		
Is it hard for me to give of my time if it does not benefit me?		
Do I criticise people?		
Do I think I am better than others?		
Am I colour conscious?		
Do I treat people of a lighter complexion better those of a darker complexion?		
Do I have goals?		
When last have I done something for the first time and what was it?		
Do I exercise manners?		
Do I show compassion?		
Do I respect all persons?		
Do I exercise limitations?		
Am I willing to learn from others?		

There is no score after the taking of this questionnaire. There is no judgment or condemnation as a result of the answers chosen. This is a form of introspection, a way for you to analyse yourself to assess what changes you, as a person, need to formulate to assist in the creation of a better you. There are no right or wrong answers, merely honest ones. Therefore, there are suggestions to assist where changes need to be made.

SUGGESTIONS

- Understand your limitations and avoid situations where you do not possess some measure of control
- Walk away from arguments
- Find the positive in someone in contrast to the negative
- Help someone
- Support others
- Give compliments
- Talk to yourself daily and make positive confessions
- Be observant
- Listen before you speak
- Use your time wisely
- Do not let the pains from the past dictate your future
- Control your reactions
- Change your perceptions
- Be empathic towards others
- Exercise forgiveness

- Acknowledge that you are not perfect
- Understand that you are in competition only with yourself
- Therefore, try to beat your best efforts.

Look around you. Observe the people closest to you first and verify whether you saw the mechanisms put into place hundreds of years ago, still manifesting themselves in today's society. This might be simple and hidden behind a greeting such as "my nigger how you doing?" Then, do some introspection and analyse yourself, your thoughts, your words and your actions and put great effort into changing them where necessary.

Whatever it may be, identify the mental chains that still hold you and break them. Peace and love starts and ends with you and you have to love and live in peace with yourself before you can effectively love and live in peace with another. "If you do not know love and peace, how then can you exercise it?"

CHAPTER FOURTEEN
SHARING THE VISION
FINAL DESTINATION

I t is time for us to put an end to all the excuses, lies and complaints. Stop using the middle passage as an excuse to continue living in mediocrity. No longer are we allowed to be at the receiving end of the slave master's whip, believing that nothing can be done about it. The word "defeated" should no longer be used to describe how one feels about their present situation. Fear and negativity should be placed in the background as one forges ahead to a new horizon while living in peace and love.

With this new-found strength, comes great responsibility. Knowledge is now your super power, as with it, insurmountable tasks become surmountable and afford a wider variety of choices to manoeuvre through frustrating situations as they arise. With knowledge, comes a contemporary way of thinking, an advanced and renewed consciousness. One becomes empowered to perform extraordinary works where considerable results can be achieved. Development and expansion of self and a people, are now possible because of knowledge.

Therefore, the responsibility is on you to distribute the wealth of knowledge, thereby assisting others in achieving this renewed level of consciousness. In Hosea 4:6, we are cautioned that a people can perish for having a lack of knowledge. The rise or fall of a people depends on how knowledgeable they are and the application and utilisation of this consciousness to benefit the needs of the people.

One needs to now mentally envisage and focus on the desired destination (your goals as an individual and as a united race) and no longer emphasise the journey taken to get to their present position. We are aware of the journey, and we thank our ancestors for their sacrifices. Now, we must forge ahead to ensure that their sacrifices were not in vain.

If one wants to be at that desired destination, then one must visualise it in one's mind as clearly as one sees a tree or a chair. Subsequently, one must desire it so badly that even though it's in one's mind, one can almost touch it. Finally, one must employ mechanisms towards achieving this goal and work assiduously towards achieving it. It really is as easy as 1-2-3.

1. Visualise your goal

2. Put mechanisms in place to achieve it

3. Execute

We know the important things, namely who we are and where we came from. Now, we need to concentrate on the destination and how we intend to get there. We do not need to be distracted the by the other, sometimes insignificant details. We do not, at this juncture, need to be stuck like a spinning top, in one location continually having the same nostalgic discussions while fighting over minor details about the past when there is no clear picture of how we intend to move forward with no new charted course in mind. To whom much is given, much is expected as we are no longer in darkness. Currently, we know and now we see the light. We have read, researched, analysed, and at this moment it is time for the gathered knowledge to be exercised.

The time has come for us to stop passing the buck as it ends here with you and me, and it is up to us to control and change our present situation. As a people, we must love each other in the truest sense of the word and understand that with unity comes strength. We must accept that we are a unique race that is powerful and resilient. There-fore, together we can move mountains. Therefore, we must:

- Stop the hate
- Stop the killing
- Support businesses owned by our brothers and sisters.
- Start cottage industries and rely on ourselves.
- Support each other
- Stop the crabs-in-a-barrel syndrome

No more excuses or believing of lies to keep us in a stagnated state. We are now ready to take the bull by the horns and see things through new eyes, fearless eyes, a new consciousness. Let us now live in peace and love.

Living in peace and love as an African dark-skinned person, means supporting and not trying to sabotage each other, not harbouring hate against each other or self, not gossiping about each other or hurting each other. Living in peace and love is helping each other and pulling each other up on this journey called life. What one desires for self, one should want for their brothers and sisters, friends and even foes. If everyone exercises it, then it won't seem like an arduous journey to nowhere. But it must begin somewhere, and it must begin with someone—why not you? We have exercised bandwagonism on many occasions by liking and sharing posts on Facebook and other social networks to raise awareness of some kind but have done nothing to help with the cause. Let us raise awareness of this renewed consciousness by sharing it with others and exercising it daily. Let us not only raise awareness but let's help the cause by first changing the way we think and act.

This dark race has been the victim of many atrocities over the years, but all is not lost. We can unite and help each other to throw off the debris that has kept this race buried for far too long. Think of this beautiful race as a body, where if a limb is distressed, the body does not abandon the limb but sends signals from the brain for it (the body) to function properly and assist the distressed area until it achieves maximum functionality.

We need to understand that there is no one else genuinely willing to assist us, and therefore, we need to assist ourselves. We need to unite and stop the self-hating rituals, drive-by shootings, tribalism, colonialism, imperialism, wars, selling of narcotics to our brothers and sisters, robberies, abandoning our children, neglecting our women, etc. Can one not strive to be this way and to find this type of peace? Let us all exercise peace and love and let it become a way of life and understand that it will take effort to accomplish this.

CHAPTER FIFTEEN

LIVING IN PEACE AND LOVE

THE ART OF UNSELFISHNESS

Peace is tranquillity, harmony, friendship, goodwill, non-violence and non-aggression. This is when people are able to resolve conflicts and work together to improve the quality of their lives. Peace is recognised when fairness is exercised, equality is understood, seeking each other's well-being is a way of life and when gender and ethnicity are no longer used as barriers.

With this type of understanding of the meaning of the word peace comes an inner peace, a peace of mind, a peace that passes every understanding. This should allow us to see things from a different perspective and give us the knowledge to handle things differently. Love, on the other hand, is a bit complex and difficult for some to comprehend or define.

It is a combination of different feelings or states. It can be classified as a virtue representing kindness or compassion and, in some instances, can be classified as an emotion or an attachment. Biblically, 1 Corinthians 13:4-7 describes love as being patient and kind. It does not envy or boast nor is it proud. It does not dishonour others, is not self- seeking or easily angered, and it keeps no records of wrong. It does not delight in evil but rejoices in truth. It always protects, trusts and perseveres.

Living in peace and love is not saying "I love my brothers and sisters." it's more than just giving a donation to a charity once a year and going away with the feeling that you made a significant difference in the world and that you are not required to do more.

Living in peace and love is a lifestyle—all day, every day. Living in peace and love means loving yourself, no self-hating. It is loving who you are, the struggles that brought you to this present point in life, loving who you have become over the years, loving what you and your fore parents stood for, loving your look, your complexion, your nose, your eyes, your skin and your hair. It's loving yourself as a person, loving your accomplishments, and it ends with you not wanting to be someone else.

Living in peace and love is loving others even though they may seem unlovable. It's loving in spite of everything society hurls at you. It is learning to give to another, be it your time, smile, support, knowledge, expertise or finances. It is a sacrifice and it is loving your neighbour as you love yourself. It is understanding and accepting who you are. This notion of love brings value to our lives and gives us a feeling of security and happiness. It is not the opposite of hate but goes deeper than that.

Love does not change or fluctuate based upon the circumstances surrounding it, and therefore, it can be said that love can be learned. There are many different types of love. Some examples are:

A PARENT'S LOVE FOR A CHILD: A child may perform acts deemed wrong, but a parent will not stop loving the child or love the child any less because of this. This is real, healthy love, and it is unchanging and constant.

LOVE IN SPITE OF DEATH: Many people may have experienced the death of a loved one at some point. However, the love and admiration for that person does not die. This is Real, Healthy love and is proof that love is unchanging and constant.

LOVE OF THINGS: We all know the attachment men have to their cars, trucks and bikes. We can identify with the hours they spend washing, polishing, cleaning and even at times talking to these objects.

As a matter of fact, the way some men speak about these objects makes one believe that the breath of life was blown into it.

One would hear things like, "her engine is purring," "my baby opened out on the highway and made me proud" or perhaps "listen to her engine roar." They love their vehicle and when it begins to malfunction, they painstakingly spend hours searching to find the problems and repair them.

Even after the car is gone, they speak of it lovingly to those who will listen. They speak of their first car as though it were the love of their life.

This is real love—it is unchanging and constant. Real, healthy love can be learned by anyone and therefore, exercised by all of us as there is no excuse or benefit to us for harbouring hate.

Living in peace and love is not an unrealistic, pie in the sky, unreachable goal. It is within our grasp and closer than we may think. The discernment of how the lack of this type of love affects our development and survival as a people is the ultimate goal. Changing the way we operate and the way we think after we attain this understanding, will be the ultimate bonus.

SELF-CONTROL

Change is not always easy. Therefore, when asked to "change" be it your way of thinking, the way you dress, the way you deal with situations or even your toothbrush it sometimes is an act destined for failure dependent on the mindset of the individual on the receiving end of the request.

When one thinks of change, they automatically see it as having to give up on this person that they spent their entire life strengthening and creating and now having to be someone else—starting over. Starting over is viewed as a negative, backward act and this is psychologically met with mental barricades and ultimately resistance. In some instances, when a person is asked to change, this really is not what was needed initially.

Therefore, change, as good and as important as it is, should be discussed at length and analysed before being executed. Sometimes people are asked to change when, in fact, they should have been asked to be more controlled.

Reasonably, once viewed in this light, the request will be met with resistance and may not be even attempted. Oftentimes requests for changes are made and in reality, that was not what the person making the request really wanted. We, therefore, need to be cognisant of the fact that it's not so much what we ask but how we ask it that makes the difference in whether we are met with opposition or willingness. Also, we need to be aware of our requests and verify whether we are being unreasonable and/or bold. Ask yourself if your request is really what you want.

How do we exercise control? This answer comes when a person has a clearer understanding of "self" and when one has elevated their consciousness to a point where they see things through different eyes. It comes when a per- son can understand that they are in control of the things that happen to them, be it positive or negative and can change situations simply by the way, they react.

When one realises that turning the other cheek is not a sign of weakness or a cowardly act but instead, an act of strength and maturity by manipulating the situation to give more power, only then, can one understand what control really is. It really is very simple—control the way you behave when faced with a situation and undoubtedly, change the situation.

Further, we need to accept that there are things we can and cannot control. The Oxford dictionary defines control as having the power to influence or direct people's behaviour or course of events. Seeing that this is true, then it is an undeniable fact that directing your behaviour and charting your own course should be an easy task.

You will not prevent yourself from doing the things you want to do. One also needs to understand the difference between being accountable and being held accountable for certain actions or situations before attempts are made to control "self."

A person who is accountable does not have to be reminded of their duty but realises and accepts the fact that they are responsible for certain things and accountable to someone. A person who is held accountable for something needs to be persuaded and/or disciplined, maybe even threatened to perform positively and may still, after that, believe that they are not answerable to anyone.

In the Serenity Prayer, one asks for God to grant the serenity to accept the things they cannot change, courage to change the things they can and wisdom to know the difference. There are things we can and cannot control, things we can and cannot change, but we must be able to identify both.

THINGS YOU CAN CONTROL

YOUR BEHAVIOUR: How you react to a situation determines how far the situation could possibly reach and the results of it. How you treat someone determines how they will treat you. How you behave will determine how persons view you. How you speak, and your deportation will determine the authority you hold. Your integrity, drive and commitment can all be classified under your behaviour.

HOW YOU USE YOUR GIFTS: If one has a charismatic personality and can encourage people to do things they either do not want to do or may not have executed had they not been coerced, then this is a gift and how one uses this is what will be questioned. Would one use this to do positive or negative things?

HOW YOU SPEND YOUR TIME: Time is important and seems as though it sometimes slips through our fingers. One minute a child is a baby, and it's as though you only get the opportunity to blink before they become an adult. This is why you are urged to take the time to spend with friends and family.

YOUR HEALTH: If you eat unhealthy foods when you are younger you have to be prepared for the disadvantages of same later in your life—clogged arteries, joint pains, acid reflux from skipping meals, etc.

The older folks say: "You are what you eat," and this is true. Your health is your responsibility.

YOUR HABITS: You can choose to do the right things. The habits you form are your choice and the choices you make are your responsibility. Think about how your habits and your choices affect you and by extension, those around you.

YOUR BELIEFS AND VALUES: Ultimately, your belief system and the values you exhibit are things only you can control. No-one can make you believe what you don't and no-one can change your value system.

YOUR IMAGE: You have the ability to control the way people see you. If they take you for a big joke, or if they see you as successful, happy, authoritative or simple, depends on how you first see yourself. Therefore, by integrating the proper mechanisms to shape yourself will alter the way others will view you

YOUR TOLERANCE: An irritating person should not be able to make you act in a disturbing manner towards them. This world is made up of many different people with many different personalities. It makes the world a little more interesting, but sometimes you are either lucky or unlucky to come into contact with persons who will test the extent of your resolve. This is a test you can pass as you are the only person who should be allowed to "get under your skin."

YOUR MOOD: Do not allow anyone to have control over you to the extent where your feelings, your mood or your thoughts are manipulated like the strings of a puppet. No person or situation should determine whether you are happy or sad; only you should control this.

GOALS: Only you know what you want out of life and only you will have that drive or motivation to stick to your goals in order to achieve them.

THINGS YOU HAVE NO CONTROL OVER

WHAT PEOPLE THINK: This cannot be controlled nor should one try to sway the thoughts of another. Another person's thoughts do not and should not concern you, especially if it was kept within the confines of their mind. Controlling others or trying to dominate others and their thoughts are signs of inadequacies of self. There are several reasons one would attempt to control another, and these may include one or more than one of the following reasons:

- Fear of being abandoned
- A desire to feel superior
- To prove it can be done
- A feeling of helplessness

THE PAST: The past is just that—the past. It is gone and will not return, so dwelling on things that have already transpired makes little or no sense. One has no control over things that happened, but one does have control over things that will happen.

THE WEATHER: How many times have you washed and polished your vehicle and driven out of the yard only to be caught in a downpour of rain? Maybe you were planning an event for months and on the day of the event, rain ruined it. One cannot control the weather, and we are actually at its mercy.

PEOPLE WHO DO NOT WANT TO CHANGE: If a person comes to you and says, "Will you help me?" only then will that person accept your assistance. If help was not requested and there is no desire for change, then you cannot help this person, and you have no control over this.

CHAPTER SIXTEEN

THE ART OF REASONING

SEEING THINGS THROUGH DIFFERENT EYES

Oftentimes, we take for granted the little things that will bring joy, peace, hope and love into our lives and the lives of others. Something as simple as a compliment can bring a genuine smile to the lips of another person. But over the years, we have become so selfish and desensitised to the pains of humanity, that we overlook the simple things that make us human. We do not take the time to see things through different eyes. We seem to always be in a rush to jump to conclusions and act without knowledge.

That old adage comes to mind: "Take time to slow down and smell the roses" but it's more than simply smelling a flower. It's about slowing down to enjoy your family, or to notice your spouse or significant other. It's about enjoying scenery, taking a long drive to new places, and it's about knowing more than just the club. This is the reason why monitoring the shows we view, the clips we are exposed to on social networks and the conversations we glean from are so important for our development.

Regretfully, we are desensitised to death, people's pain, emotions, love, and we are slowly losing the very essence of our humanity. "If we do not know what we desire, then how can we know what to give" The reality is that many of us do not know what desire is or the power it holds.

Orthodox rabbi Rav Ashlag once said: "Humans would not twitch a single finger if not for some inner desire." International author and speaker Yehuda Berg wrote—Desire is the stuff we're made of. It is our existence. Desire is what drives us. It is what makes us tick. We are desires on foot, constantly seeking to fulfil our own cravings. Our hearts beat, our blood flows, our bodies move solely because there's a desire and urge seeking to be fulfilled."

INTROSPECTION: Look into yourself for a brief moment and answer the following question—"What do I want to give to another person"? A simple definition of giving is being able to transfer freely, the possession of something to someone. Indubitably, some of you have not come up with a response as most people believe they really only have enough to sustain themselves and in such a trying time, cannot afford to render assistance to others.

Others may say that people who have not acquired much in their lifetime should get up and be responsible for achieving their own goals. They may probably use a scripture quoted in their religious books to justify their erroneous and selfish statements and behaviour.

A simple statement made years ago by someone who probably never got enough credit for saying it, is one of the most abused statements ever uttered, as it is constantly oft-repeated, yet people do not exercise it. But it offers most sound advice—"Give a man a fish and feed him for a day. Teach a man to fish and feed him for a lifetime." If one feeds a man for a day by just giving him a fish daily, that man will only be able to eat during the day or days that food is provided but if one teaches him how to fish, he will in turn go out and fish to ensure he eats daily. He will now have a new ability, self-worth and pride and can employ same in making himself marketable.

Is it possible that some people are still in the business of slavery, not wanting to empower another individual for fear that persons will no longer be under their control as one sadistically dangles a "fish" for training purposes as one would train an animal and give it treats as a reward for good behaviour? Is it that some people like the power of knowing the future of another person's existence is in the palm of their hand and enjoy exercising their "God Complex"?

It is time, if we indeed want change, that we go back to being our brother's keeper, respect each other and stop the selfishness.

We learned over the years that respect is earned and that one must become someone worth respecting in order to be respected. Be a leader, be successful and be respected. I do not agree with this statement, and I often wonder why society tries to quantify everything, everyone and every situation with the same measuring tool when we know that this cannot be done and should be discontinued.

Lack of respect is one of the main reasons behind the collapse of many organisations, friendships, relationships, community groups, religious orders, etc. Since we have been programmed to respect only those in authority, we neglect to show any form of respect to the persons we consider less authoritative. We disregard their contribution to society and act as though they are virtually invisible. We pay no attention to the "behind the scenes" people who make the leader's dream a reality.

IF WE ALL LEAD THEN WHO WILL FOLLOW?

We need to be cognisant of the fact that these "non-leaders" have valid contributions and ideas. Imagine for a moment if the garbage collectors stopped collecting your garbage what utter mess the place would be and what chaos would arise.

Think about, if you will, the health implications of leaving rotted garbage on the streets. Imagine the germs that would be incubated, growing and multiplying in that environment, the flies, cockroaches, and rats that would have a frenzy in and around that mess.

However, we find it easy to disrespect these unrecognised heroes and most times not even a kind word is uttered to them. Garbage truck attendants on pick-up duty have to run miles behind this smelly truck picking up the worm-infested garbage bags you leave for them. They are vulnerable to not just diseases but to being hurt in various ways such as infections, respiratory damage, parasites like hookworm, tapeworms and roundworms, being pricked by needles or cut by broken bottles, etc.

Having regard to the dangers faced by garbage men and the fact that they have thrown caution to the wind in an attempt to assist and keep you safe, how hard is it to show them the respect they deserve?

Have you ever considered being nice to the taxi driver? Their job is already a stressful one, and most times does not offer the financial security needed to cover the needs (not wants) of the people dedicated to doing this job. Further, coupled with the fact that it is considered a menial job by society's standards, one would find it hard to keep self-motivated everyday providing this service to whom they rightfully in most cases consider, ungrateful people. It is also one of the most dangerous occupations in the world and whenever a taxi driver buckles their seat belt, his or her life is put at risk. In 2005, taxi drivers were estimated to be 18 times more likely to die on the job than any other working American.

The Occupational Safety and Health Administration (OSHA) reported in the year 2000 that 183.8 drivers per 1000 were injured from assault or other violent acts and in the same year warned about the dangers of driving a taxi. Yet many people, without thinking of the dangers taxi drivers are exposed to daily, choose to show little or no respect for them. Once one can methodically scrutinise these types of jobs and ascertain the negative impact their absence would have on society then respecting them and what they do should come easily.

Many of us, if we be honest, would not be able to do for ourselves what these persons have mastered and can do for us and for this reason, they deserve to be respected. Society should by now be running like a well-oiled machine and the reason it does not is because we lack respect for each other.

Scrutinise the following list of what are considered mediocre jobs in society and ponder how their absence would affect your daily routine, be it negatively or positively.

- The grocery attendant
- The store clerk
- The fish vendor
- The mailman
- The secretary
- The maxi/taxi touts.
- The maid
- The custodian
- The mechanic
- The drain cleaners
- The gardener
- The painter
- The tyre attendant
- The gas station attendant
- The security guard

The law of reciprocity states that once you give it comes back to you, yet we do not believe that giving respect is part of that law. Are we then to believe that it is a convenient law? No, it isn't. Therefore, respect the people around you and they will in turn reciprocate. By extension, you would have done your part in making a positive impact on the lives of others.

Remember the adage: "You can catch more flies with honey than with vinegar." The law of reciprocity encourages us to give with the promise that it will be given back to us. If you are kind to someone, they in return will be nice to you. If you share with someone, they will share with you. If you assist someone, then you too will be assisted. It sounds a lot like catching more flies with honey than with vinegar. These aphorisms from long ago possesses a wealth of knowledge that we could garner and implement to create a better world but many do not examine these statements properly or in their entirety for a holistic understanding of their meaning. Rather, they extract the parts that are convenient to them. People usually look for this law to be consummated by them receiving material gain for helping people This, however, is the "what's in it for me" attitude that is displayed when, in fact, the deed should have been executed genuinely.

Many people don't appreciate or don't realise when they have "received returns" based on this principle of giving. For example, the good deed you did by offering your neighbour a meal could be returned by an adult being vigilant and paying attention to your child or children. The law of reciprocity is comparable to one attracting positive energy or positive vibrations by executing a positive act. Whatever someone requires at the point of executing a deed of kindness, whether consciously or subconsciously, is what is received.

When one sincerely performs a good deed as giving to charity, spending time with family, holding someone's hand to cross the street, fixing a bike chain for a child, giving directions to the lost or buying groceries for the poor—once the act is genuinely discharged, one will be rewarded with the desires of their heart at the point in time. If your desire at the point in time is your child's safe arrival from school, then this is what your energy will be channelled towards achieving and will be deemed the desires of your heart at that particular time, and this is what you will receive. The possibilities are endless.

Therefore, it makes perfect sense to treat others the way we would like to be treated. Instead of thinking "What's in it for me?" perhaps one can now ask: "What if it happened to me?" Positive thoughts breed positive actions and have been associated over the years with being linked to improving an overall healthier individual. Being positive is about seeing your glass as half full in contrast to seeing it half empty. Therefore, if we change the way we see things, inadvertently, we will succeed in changing the outcome of the situation completely.

Don't be afraid to talk to yourself and periodically give yourself the "pep talks" or motivational speeches that are often a prerequisite for a successful individual as you are required to be your biggest cheerleader. You need to see things into fruition, see the transformation and see the growth and remember that nothing changes until you refashion it. Remember always, that no one can "fight you down" without your permission. Their negativity, unless accepted and internalised by you, has no effect on your success or failure.

CHAPTER SEVENTEEN

WHAT'S IN IT FOR ME?

LEARNING EMPATHY

Change begins with you. It should not be viewed as an onerous task to offer a person a glass of water or a plate of food. You may be surprised at the positive response you may receive. For some, the acceptance of such an offer may come because they do not know where their next meal will come from.

The definition of selfishness is the inability to positively contribute without the possibility of gain. Selfish persons have mastered the art of the four E's

1. **Explore**–Search for friends
2. **Exploit**–Unfairly use friends
3. **Extract**–Take all they can from friends
4. **Eradicate**–Get rid of friends

Egocentric people cannot identify with the fact that they are selfish unless it is brought to their attention and in some cases even when they are made aware of this fact, they choose to devise excuses for and justify their selfishness. Nevertheless, in their time of introspection, they may employ the three A's in order for change to take place in their lives.

1. Awareness: This is done by comparison of virtues with those around them.

2. Acknowledgement: Admitting that they are guilty of being selfish.

3. Admission: Confessing and implementing systems to change it.

SAFETY AND SECURITY

You have a desire to feel safe and forge ahead with a master plan to ensure that this becomes a reality. You work hard to put mechanisms in place for the safety and security you, and your family enjoy. Congratulations.

Earlier in the book, we spoke about humanity losing its essence and being desensitised to the basics. The essence of humanity cannot be described in a paragraph, but there are a few basic qualities that define the essence of humanity.

- It is the ability to show love, compassion, care and concern for others.
- It is the ability to connect with persons on different levels.
- It is the ability to have amazing memories.
- It is the ability to be charitable.

Over time and having lost the ability to be empathetic towards each other, humans have become selfish creatures and have forgot- ten about being their brother's keeper. Too many of us refuse to extend ourselves to others and don't care about the quandary someone may have gotten themselves into which could have been avoided with proper advice. People have now taken a position where they believe what transpires with another person has nothing to do with them. How wrong and selfish that statement truly is. One should be empathetic towards another's pain as exercising empathy assists with understanding self thereby promoting growth and healing. When someone understands themselves, they become happier, more tolerant, enjoy life more, exercise control, think more positively and make better decisions.

Marshall Rosenberg, an American psychologist, mediator, author and teacher said: "Time and again, people transcend the paralysing effects of psychological pain when they have sufficient contact with someone who can hear them empathically." Spiritual leader, poet and peace activist Thich Nhat Hanh said: "Deep listening is the kind that can help relieve the suffering of another person. You can call it compassionate listening. You listen with only one purpose: to help him or her to empty his heart."

According to the Centre for Building a Culture of Empathy, empathy has several defining characteristics:

- It fosters emotional and physical health and well-being.
- It gives a sense of identity

- It heals painful psychological problems
- It fosters good, pleasurable and positive feelings.
- Is the active ingredient in conflict resolution
- Is a source of creativity, innovation and transformative action
- Is a gateway to, and supports, socially desirable values
- It expands our perspectives
- It helps us find and meet our needs, values and aspirations
- It increases helping and altruistic behaviour (Batson et al., 1987; Eisenburg & Miller, 1987; Krebs, 1975; Toi & Batson, 1982)
- Has many benefits in specific context

Sue Gerhardt, author of "Why Love Matters?'" writes: "Empathy is one of the highest human skills and holds families and societies together. Feeling connected to other people is probably the deepest satisfaction we will ever know. How terrible for children who are being brought up without that capacity".

We may not be aware of the trials another person has encountered simply because people have mastered the ability to mask their pain/hardship and usually agonise in silence. Some of those people struggle or have tried on countless occasions to change their situations but failed, either because they did not know how or where to start or may have met insuperable challenges along the way.

However, there are times we may have been aware of the tribulations endured by others as we may have been able to see it as plainly as we see the tree growing in the yard or the car that is parked on the side of the street. Even so, we selfishly enshroud ourselves in our own lives and become individuals who are no longer concerned about humanity, when, in fact, instance like these where we could lend assistance to someone in need is where we could have exercised being our brother's keeper.

No more do people know the names of their neighbours, what they drive or how many people occupy their homes. No longer is a village allowed to raise a child and yet we wonder why the children go astray. No longer do persons forge lasting relationships with their neighbours or lend a helping hand. Selfishness seems to be the order of the day and the root from which the breakdown in society originates.

The healthy, positive relationships we forge allow us to diffuse our own selfishness by enabling us to treat others the way we want to be treated. We speak to others the way we want to be spoken to. We reason with others to diffuse a situation that could have potentially been volatile. We extend respect to others regardless of age, race, job security, or political affiliation. We become our brother's keeper, and in so doing, we understand the importance of respect.

Should we not make a genuine attempt at being empathetic to others who need to relieve their mental suffering? With this new evidence before us describing in detail the benefits of exercising empathy, we can therefore recognise that an ounce of kindness goes a long way benefiting both the person on the receiving end as well as the person exercising empathy. Being nice to someone or exercising empathy does not come with a cost attached but the benefit derived from this practice is priceless.

CHAPTER EIGHTEEN

FREEDOM

BREAKING THE CHAINS OF
SELF-INFLICTED SLAVERY

So you got a job, a career, a profession, your occupation. It might be your dream job or a job that simply pays the bills and offers you some security and comfort but the reality is you have a job, your very own job that some others wished they had. This job security affords you the convenience of being able to plan for the future and the serenity of living a relatively comfortable life.

To some, this job would have been earned, as many hours of hard work and dedication made it possible to acquire, while for others, it's a miracle, as a miracle seems impossible to achieve but happens anyway. Oftentimes, people find themselves guilty of placing more emphasis on the job than any other aspect of their lives and because of this, their lives are centred around the job and not on what truly matters, which is family.

It is arguable that without a job, nothing else would be made possible, but is it acceptable to sacrifice everything else in an attempt to secure and maintain a job? Some start to become "slaves" to their occupation of choice and do not recognise their shackles. It becomes the drug of choice, addictive, and holds them captive. The job requires a person to be in attendance at a particular time and leave at a stipulated time.

The divide between good, efficient, reliable employee and slave is sometimes crossed and masked by persons being described as efficient, always on call and dedicated. These job slaves often times skip lunch, stay for many hours after the stipulated leaving time (without compensation), persons in positions of authority are not patient and do not exercise leniency, and the list can be far reaching.

Devoting oneself to the job to the extent where one can be described as a slave can result in an individual becoming unrecognisable, losing their consciousness, compromising their standards and morals. It can also result in poor health issues, accepting loneliness for a sizeable pay increase, changing one's personality to correspond with society's perception of what said personality should be, losing family and relationships and finally losing self.

Is one prepared to accept these losses just to prove to others that they "made it" and that their years of dedication were not in vain? Is one prepared to admit and accept that a happy existence is replaceable by the love of money? I firmly believe that it is erroneous to think that one would prefer to be unhappy and miserable while crying in an expensive car than to be living happily while driving a more economical car. Therefore, you have to ask yourself: "Does humanity's ego outweigh its virtue?"

EVERYTHING IN DEGREES

The interpretation of the following phrase is important as we need to take stock of our actions and the way we reason or rationalise things— Everything in degrees. As much as we would like to ignorantly deny that abuse goes further than just the physical, it does and sadly, in some instances, some people are guilty of inflicting abuse even on themselves.

Indulging in too much of anything can be considered abuse, especially when the gratification is at the risk of one's development. Too much partying can weaken the body at rapid speeds causing one to age quickly. It is as a result of not getting enough rest, which is necessary to the development and proper performance of the body and mind.

This type of self-inflicted abuse can leave the door open for sickness and diseases in some instances. When the mind is tired, the performance level is inhibited, one's reaction time is delayed and the ability to reason is limited. A tired body and mind, is a stressed body and mind.

Too much work can result in the losses previously discussed in a prior chapter but gave a mental picture of how individuals, and their families have been affected. The following scenario gives an additional aspect to this topic. A person leaves for work at 5 am to eradicate the prospect of getting entangled in traffic to start their workday which begins at 8 am and ends at 4 pm, but does not get home until after 7 pm because of traffic.

Tired and mentally drained, they arrive home with a desire to not be disturbed after a long, stressful day at work. Then they can perform the mental purging ritual (watch television, play a video game, wash or fix the car, chat online) that affords them the ability to keep their sanity. Then they get ready for bed about 9.30 pm as they have to be well-rested for the day ahead which begins at 4 am.

A shower and dinner might take approximately an hour and watching a show on the television which they worked hard to purchase, might take about an hour. This just leaves one with about half of an hour to spend with their children and their spouse.

Sadly, but realistically, the kids might already be asleep and would undoubtedly be asleep when they leave in the morning. The partner is feeling rejected and taken for granted and allows negative thoughts to consume their mind based on the actions presented. Over time, this complicated and mundane routine pushes a wedge between couples and causes them to drift independently, resulting in the tearing apart of families. This leaves one party thinking their sacrifices and efforts are in vain and unappreciated yet had to be made as it was a necessary "evil."

Situations like these propel the individual to drown their discontent in the whirlpool that the job has become, working longer hours. These are just two examples of self-inflicted abuse.

Let us now try to identify instances where we "self-abuse" and put limits on the things we engage in. Reflect on the phrase "everything in degrees" and understand that change begins with you.

Consider doing the following:

- **Limit your phone time**–someone may want your attention.

- **Limit your party time**–think about your health and the repercussions of abusing your mind and body.

- **Limit your work time**–acknowledge your behaviour and know that you are replaceable. Do not take the job home with you and remember someone is excitedly awaiting your return. Think about how your actions affect them.

- **Limit your television time**—abusing this can result in poor eyesight and headaches, which in turn affects your mood. Go out and experience what the real world has to offer and ask yourself when did you last experience something for the first time.

Even though this list may be a summarised guideline of the things people are guilty of, you can sit in your quiet time and make a more comprehensive list in your quest to create a better you. Remember always that if we treat each other the way, we want to be treated the world would be a better place. Moreover, change begins with you.

Therefore, put down your belief system for a brief moment consider, investigate and process the following statement "If we treat each other the way we want to be treated, then the world would be a better place. "One would marvel at how profound a statement it is, and I urge you, the reader, to not just read and enjoy the contents of this book but to understand the principles and teachings brought forth and integrate them into your daily lives until they become second nature.

REFERENCES

Madam Ambassador. "History Black Pioneers." Pinterest. N.p., 11 Feb. 2013. Web.

"African American Inventors." Www.vidinfo.org. N.p., n.d. Web.

"African Societies and the Beginning of the Atlantic Slave Trade" (article) Khan Academy. N.p., n.d. Web.

"Africans Sold Their Own People as Slaves" Abagond. N.p., 27 Aug. 2015. Web.

"The Capture and Sale of Enslaved Africans." National Museums Liverpool. N.p., n.d. Web.

Child Soldiers International. N.p., n.d. Web.

"Christopher Columbus." Biography.com. A&E Networks Television, 1 Aug. 2017. Web.

"Emmett Till." Biography.com. A&E Networks Television,
28 Apr. 2017. Web.

"Facts on Human Trafficking and Sex Slavery | Soroptimist." Soroptimist – Women's Organization – Volunteer Organizations. N.p., n.d. Web.

"The Final Call." Willie Lynch Letter: The Making of a Slave. N.p., n.d. Web.

Gluck, Samantha. "Effects of Rape: Psychological and Physical Effects of Rape" HealthyPlace. N.p., n.d. Web.

Haitian Revolution (1791-1804) | The Black Past: Remembered and Reclaimed. N.p., n.d. Web.

"History: Abolition." BBC. BBC, n.d. Web.

"Medgar Evers." History.com. A&E Television Networks, 2009.

"Nat Turner." History.com. A&E Television Networks, 2009

"IIF News Releases." U.S. Bureau of Labor Statistics. U.S. Bureau of Labor Statistics, n.d. Web.

Initiative, Prison Policy. "Research about Criminal Justice Is- sues:." Prison Research Index - What's New All | Prison Policy Initiative. N.p., n.d. Web.

ISBN:1459602285 - Google Search. N.p., n.d. Web.

James A. Levine (Author). "Get Up! Why Your Chair Is Killing You and What You Can Do About It" (9781137278999) James A. Levine: Books. N.p., n.d. Web.

Lion, Couer De. "The Joseph Anointing". N.p., n.d. Web.

"Martin Luther King Jr." Nobelprize.org. N.p., n.d. Web.

"The Reemergence of The KKK." Khan Academy. N.p., n.d. Web. Revolvy, LLC. "List of countries by incarceration rate" on Revolvy.com." Revolvy. N.p., n.d. Web.

"Rosa Parks." Biography.com. A&E Networks Television, 07 Aug. 2017. Web.

"Sam Sharpe and the Baptist War Sped up Emancipation." News | Jamaica Gleaner. N.p., n.d. Web.

"A Short History of Slavery and Sugar Cane in Jamaica." The Official Globe Trekker Website. N.p., n.d. Web.

"Slavery." Aframroots. N.p., n.d. Web.

"Slavery in the Chocolate Industry." CSGlobe. N.p., 04 May 2017. Web.

"South African Blacks Forced To Deal With Issue Of Tribalism." Tribunedigital-chicagotribune. N.p., 10 Sept. 1990. Web.

"Top 10 African American Inventors." Listverse. N.p., 11 June 2014. Web.

"Top 10 Caribbean Athletes Of All-Time." Caribbean & Co. N.p., 19 Mar. 2016. Web.

"Tunisia: Constantine Declared as Arab Cultural Capital." The North Africa Post. N.p., 31 Dec. 2012. Web.

Watson, Dr Karl. "History - British History in Depth: Slavery and Economy in Barbados." BBC. BBC, 17 Feb. 2011. Web.

"Yehuda Berg Quotes." BrainyQuote. Xplore, n.d. Web.

Made in the USA
Middletown, DE
04 October 2022